Dr. Linda S

Now I Get It!

Totally Sensational Advice For
Living and Loving

Outskirts Press, Inc.
Denver, Colorado

NOW I GET IT!
Totally Sensational Advice for Living and Loving

Outskirts Press
http://www.outskirtspress.com

ISBN-10: 1-59800-887-0
ISBN-13: 978-1-59800-887-6

Printed in the United States of America

DEDICATION

To Ron Goodrich:
> My husband and loving friend, who focuses my thoughts, soothes my anxieties, and supports me in my many creative endeavors. I will always be thankful for your fine mind, insightful editing and providing me with "a beautiful, free and intimate space."

To Brian, Naomi, Glenn, Danny & Sara:
> May your children, yet to be, brighten your world with the joy and laughter that you have brought to mine.

Books by DR. SAPADIN

-Master Your Fears: How to Triumph Over Your Worries and Get On With Your Life© (John Wiley, 2004, also published in Korean)

-It's About Time! The 6 Styles of Procrastination and How to Overcome Them© (Viking/Penguin, 1996, also published in Japanese) with Jack Maguire

-Beat Procrastination and Make the Grade: The 6 Styles of Procrastination and How Students Can Overcome Them© (Penguin, 1999) with Jack Maguire

-101 Great Ways to Improve Your Life: Chapter Title: Overcoming Resistance: What's Stopping You?© (Self-Growth.com, 2006)

For more information about these books, contact her at
www.PsychWisdom.com or DrSapadin@aol.com.

ABOUT THE AUTHOR

Linda Sapadin, Ph.D., **psychologist, author**, and **motivational speaker**, is known for her sharp insights and exceptional ability to provide timely yet timeless advice. Her specialties are helping people **build competence, enrich relationships** and **overcome self-defeating patterns of behavior.**

Dr. Sapadin has had extensive media experience, appearing on the *Today Show, National Public Radio, Voice of America* and a host of other TV and radio programs.

Her work has been **featured in** *The New York Times, USA Today, Newsday, The Washington Post, The Los Angeles Times, Cosmopolitan, Self, First, Ladies' Home Journal, Prevention, Moxie, Fitness, Redbook, Good Housekeeping, Men's Health, Bottom Line,* and many other publications.

Dr. Sapadin has been an **invited speaker** to the *Smithsonian,* the *American Psychological Association, Coopers & Lybrand, Hofstra University* and other business and educational organizations.

PsychWisdom is the name of her weekly newsletter. You can receive a free subscription to this publication by requesting one at www.PsychWisdom.com

Dr. Sapadin also writes a weekly column for the Herald chain of newspapers, published on Long Island, New York.

Now I Get It! is a collection of 62 of her inspiring, empowering and entertaining columns.

TABLE OF CONTENTS

PART 4: THE ART OF PARENTING 133

PART 5: DEALING WITH DIFFICULT PEOPLE 159

PART 6: THE CHANGE PROCESS 175

A Note to My Readers:

"My mother giving advice is like the Cookie Monster being paid to eat cookies; she's a natural!" That was Glenn's response to the New York Times reporter when he was asked to comment on his mom possibly becoming the next Ann Landers.

That was 1987. No, I didn't replace Ann Landers, but I did have my first 15 minutes of fame (well, actually my second, but that's another story). I was chosen as a finalist from more than 11,000 contestants who answered the Chicago Sun-Times' call for a replacement for Ms. Landers, when she began writing for a competitive newspaper - the Chicago Tribune.

Oh, those were heady times: a photo interview in People Magazine, lead story in New York Newsday, front page article in the New York Times, and a host of radio and print interviews. After the publicity died down, the substantial stuff started. I was offered my own advice column and call-in radio show in the Long Island area where I live. This was the best payoff for me as I had no intention of moving to Chicago – as lovely as that city is.

As I reflected on these new opportunities, I realized what a long way I had come – from being a frightened child, certain of nothing, to being a confident woman – and psychologist to boot – who knew what she was talking about and was no longer shy about sharing it with others.

Now, two decades later, my writing skills have matured; my advice giving has flourished and I've developed a unique style. My style shies away from quick quips that trump complexity – "dump your boyfriend", "quit your complaining". It also shuns an elitist approach that suggests that "I know how you should live your life, so listen to me."

Instead, my advice is based on wisdom that I've gained through the

1

years from my clinical practice, expansive readings, familiarity with psychological research and from being an acute observer of life.

My goal is to inspire readers to step outside their comfort zone, expand their minds, and augment what they 'know'. By so doing, they '**Get It!**' - becoming more aware, enlightened, and empowered. The end result: the world becomes a more complex, yet strangely enough, easier place to live.

As I write this last paragraph, a story comes to mind that is illustrative of my own recent growth. I was carrying one of my paintings to my summer apartment when a woman in the elevator commented on how much she liked the painting. When I told her it was my own art work, she replied, "Wow, that's great. I couldn't draw to save myself." I responded, "I used to think that way too, not too long ago. But then I gave it a try. I learned a few techniques, I wasn't too hard on myself, and I was surprised at how much I improved."

"Really?" she said. "Really," I replied. "Since I stepped outside my comfort zone, downplayed my 'I can't do this' message, let supportive and caring artists nurture me (thank you, Iris and Ivan), I **got it.** And not only do I now view myself as a fledgling artist, but I also appreciate great art so much more.

"Getting it" opens up doors. Of course, it's not only a new interest that can open up to you. Indeed, it's usually more profound matters, such as:
-Getting out of the victim position.
-Enriching your intimate relationships.
-Knowing how to cope with criticism.
-Learning how to speak so that you're taken seriously.
-Making sense out of the chaos of your childhood.

Being enlightened about such matters makes a difference – in how you think about yourself and in the way you live in the world. It not only empowers you, it delights you as clarity replaces confusion.

Now I Get It! is a collection of columns I've written for my website and for the Herald chain of newspapers. I've organized these columns into six parts:

Part 1. Personal Growth – Investing in your own growth is always a good idea. It expands possibilities for yourself that you may not have even known you had.
> **A Sampling:**
> *"You Don't Have To Be a Victim"*
> *"The Damaging Duo - Stress and Worry"*

Part 2. Communication – To be understood by another, we need to communicate so that the other person 'gets' us.
> **A Sampling:**
> *"Your Words Matter"*
> *"Discover Your But!"*

Part 3. Intimate Relationships – We fall in love; love is blind. Sooner or later, we regain our sight; then what?
> **A Sampling:**
> *"Couples in Conflict"*
> *"Compromises: Graciously or Grudgingly Given?"*

Part 4. The Art of Parenting – Parenting is more art than science. But like art, we need to acquire the skills that give rise to great performance.
> **A Sampling:**
> *"Entitled Kids, Defensive Parents"*
> *"Mother-Daughter Adult Relationships"*

Part 5. Dealing With Difficult People - Fasten your seat belts; you may be in for a bumpy ride as you learn the skills needed to deal with difficult personality types.

A Sampling:
"How to Argue With a Difficult Person"
"Dealing With a Passive-Aggressive Personality"

Part 6. The Change Process – You can be the recipient of the best advice. But if you pay no attention to it, are you really any better off?

A Sampling:
"Can People Really Change?"
"Psychotherapy – To Know It Is To Appreciate It"

If you're first making your acquaintance with my columns, let me welcome you to a community of readers who are bright, interesting, curious people – always willing to learn.

I'd like to invite you to visit my website at www.PsychWisdom.com or write to me at DrSapadin@aol.com.

Share with me which columns were most valuable to you, which inspired you, taught you a specific skill or helped you connect the dots of your life. Also, let me know which you didn't like or what you disagree with.

Feel free to suggest additional topics for me to write about, as I hope that this will be the first in a series of books that provides "totally sensational advice" for "totally sensational readers".

Dr. Linda Sapadin

PART 1

Personal Growth
Investing in your own growth
is always a good idea.

*There's only one corner of the universe you can be certain
of improving; and that's your own self.*

Aldous Huxley

*I know of no more encouraging fact than the unquestionable
ability of man to elevate his life by conscious endeavor.*

Henry David Thoreau

You Don't Have To Be A Victim

It's easy to feel like a victim when someone bigger, more powerful or more outspoken than you tells you what to do. You may believe that you have no other option but to do as you're told, no matter your feelings. Yet, I am here to tell you that you always have an option.

Even when you're not able to change the situation, one option that nobody can take away from you is your personal power to interpret the event anyway you'd like.

If you're stuck and don't know how to do this, turn to either the wisest person you know for advice or to the youngest person you know for creativity.

If you're wondering how a 3-year-old can teach you anything, here's an example of what my youngest son Daniel taught me when he was still in nursery school.

> Danny was a determined, self-assured little boy. He seemed to be that way from the day he was born. He knew what he liked. He knew what he wanted. He knew how to avoid being a victim.

> One day, Danny's older brothers and dad were glued to the television set for a playoff game. A bored Danny was doing everything he could to distract them from their activity. After a fair amount of warnings, we all had had it with his antics. I decided it was time to take action. Short-tempered myself, I pulled Danny down the hallway; then shoved him

into his room. (Not my finest moment, I admit.) As I slammed the door behind him, I hissed, "Now you stay there!"

Without missing a beat, Danny opened the door, slammed it in my face, shouting "You can't come in!"

> ## "You can't come in!"

As I walked away, I could only admire his moxie. Though I was powerful enough to make him stay in his room, I had no control over his personal power. Danny refused to be the victim. He reframed the situation and made it a punishment for me!

Coming from a background in which I felt easily intimidated by others, I was blown away that Danny could do this at such a young age. What a role model for me! Since then, reflecting on this incident has been my confidence booster in many a tough situation.

Now let me share with you another story about a kid who also refused to be a victim but her dad wasn't savvy enough to be impressed by her smarts.

Walter was grouchy the day he picked up 6-year-old Amelia from soccer practice. They were in the car for just 3 minutes when he noticed in the rearview mirror that Amelia had not buckled her seat belt. Walter barked, "Stop jumping around. Get that seat belt on. And sit still!"

Amelia complied. A few minutes later, however, he noticed her sitting with arms folded and an impish look on her face. Walter demanded to know what was so funny. Amelia spit it out: "You can make me sit still, but I'm still jumpin' around on the inside."

Too bad Walter didn't get it. Too bad he wasn't impressed with the fact that Amelia could comply and defy at the same time, ending up with one sensational solution. Walter just couldn't get beyond his belief that Amelia had been disrespectful. Hence, when they arrived home, she was punished for the transgression of "jumping around on the inside."

Now, what about you? Is there a situation in which you think of yourself as the helpless victim when maybe, just maybe, you can view it another way? Before you immediately say "no way, this situation is different", think of both the wisest person you know and the most creative child you know. Ask them what they think.

NOW I GET IT!

Coping With Criticism

Want to reduce the stress in your life? Want to give yourself a great gift? If you can imagine a gift as an item that is not tangible, not gift wrapped, not store bought, but, nevertheless, is something special that you receive, then I have the gift for you.

I can teach you how to hear other people's criticism in a manner that will keep you calm and let you feel empowered. So empowered, in fact, that you will have no need to become defensive, enraged, victimized or attack back.

"What are you kidding?" I hear you say. "I'm not interested in a pre-frontal lobotomy."

"Lucky for you, I never did finish the book, *"Brain Surgery for Dummies"*.

"Well then," you might reply, "how can you expect me not to be hurt when I'm criticized - especially if the criticism is unfair and designed to attack me. Besides, I'm not even sure I want to learn how to weather criticism."

Yes, I know. It would be nice if nobody ever criticized you. If you're a sensitive soul, you just don't like it. Or maybe you're strong-willed and like doing things your own way, others be damned. Or perhaps you come from an abusive home and have heard enough criticism to last you a lifetime.

Now welcome to the real world. Here we need criticism to give us feedback about how

> **"We need criticism to give us feedback about how we're doing."**

we're doing. When we shut ourselves off from what we don't want to hear, we make it more likely that problems will snowball and minor irritations will erupt into major resentments.

If you can develop the ability to hear criticism without becoming angry or defensive, good things may happen. Of course, it's easier to do this if the criticism is given in a supportive and caring manner. However, even if the criticism is harsh, habitual, or unfair, you can learn to filter out the negative aspect of the criticism while absorbing the helpful part.

First thing you must do to cope well with criticism is to keep yourself calm so that you're able to reflect on what was said instead of just being provoked to react with a counter-attack.

Once you are in a relatively calm state, ask yourself these questions:

> **What part of the criticism do I agree with?**
> (*Yup, I was selfish.*)

> **What part of the criticism do I disagree with?**
> (*I'm not always selfish.*)

> **Can I reframe the criticism?**
> (*It's not that I only care about myself. It's that I wasn't focused on you at the moment.*)

Now that you're clear in your own mind about how valid the criticism is, you can:

> **Remove the 'sting' of the criticism by adding the word 'sometimes'.**
> (*Sometimes, I'm insensitive.*)

> **Integrate the criticism with your own viewpoint on the matter.**
> (*I admit that I could be more sensitive to your feelings, but it was never my intention to hurt you.*)

NOW I GET IT!

As you filter out the hurtful part of the criticism, an amazing thing happens. You no longer have the need to be defensive or attacking.

Here are two examples of how this can be done.

Personal Example:

> **Criticizer:** "You never listen. I can't count on you. You disappointed me again."

> **You:** "I'm sorry you're angry with me. Tell me what I did that disappointed you."

> **Criticizer:** "It's what *you didn't* do. I asked you to take care of this matter last week. You knew it was important to me and yet you still didn't do it. You always do this to me. You don't care about anybody but yourself. You're so selfish."

> **You:** "I do care about you and your feelings. I admit that I often let things slide, but I don't do it deliberately. I do tend to procrastinate and I know that's not a good thing. I'll make that call and let you know when I do. I want you to be able to trust me again."

Business Example:

> **Criticizing Customer:** "You have the worst customer service in the world. I've been on hold for 20 minutes, shuttled from person to person and still nobody can answer my question. How do you people stay in business? You're all morons."

> **You:** "I understand how upset you are. We're understaffed at certain times of the day. I apologize for the delay. Please tell me how I can be of assistance to you now."

Notice that in both examples, even though the criticizer attacks, you don't become defensive nor do you counter-attack. Instead, you filter out the punitive, hurtful part of the criticism and take in the helpful part. You turn a massive assault on your personality into a minor critique of what you did or didn't do. You don't let others drag you down to their level, defeating you at the blame and shame game.

I hope you are willing to embrace my gift and revel in its benefits. Being able to cope with criticism constructively without losing your cool or your confidence is the final act of maturity.

Judging Yourself, Judging Others

Take a moment to reflect on the worst thing that you've ever done. It could be something fairly recent or way back in your past. Don't just settle for a minor faux pas. Keep thinking until you've hit upon something that was really bad.

If you cannot remember something you did that could have landed you in jail or mortified you if it had been front page news, congratulations. You are

> "...remember some shameful act of yours"

either a saint or skilled at repressing what you don't want to remember.

Now, for those of you who do remember some shameful act of yours, how do you explain it? Don't continue reading until you come up with an explanation.

Okay. Now that you have a plausible reason as to why you did what you did, let me guess what you said. Your explanation was probably similar to one of these:

> *"I had too much to drink."*
> *"I was young."*
> *"I was angry."*
> *"I wasn't thinking."*
> *"I went along with the crowd."*
>
> *"It was a stupid impulse."*
> *"I didn't know any better."*
> *"It was a dare."*
> *"I was afraid."*

"Someone told me to do it."
"I thought I was being cool."
"I was out of my mind."

Now picture someone else doing something similar today. What would be your explanation for the behavior? Being the rational person that you are, you might be tempted to think about the same reason you just mentioned for yourself. But, in reality, it's likely that your response would be radically different - especially if somebody close to you had done it.

Your response might well have sounded like this:

"What's the matter with you?"
"What kind of a person are you?"
"Don't you have any values?"
"How could you do that?"
"How could you even think that?"
"You're pathetic."

"How stupid could you be?"
"You're not the person I married."
"Didn't I teach you anything?"
"I can't even look at you."
"You gross me out."
"You're one sick puppy."

Why should one explanation be so radically different from the other?

When making a judgment about another's bad behavior, people tend to attribute **enduring personality** or **character** traits as the cause, such as he's irresponsible, she's stupid. Yet when judging our own lapses, we tend to be more tolerant. Sure, we may feel awful about what we did, but we're more likely to explain it by citing **situational** or **temporary** factors such as, a lapse in judgment, peer pressure, mood or substance abuse.

So, who is right? Is our behavior more influenced by our personality or by the situation we find ourselves in? As much as we would like to believe that we are masters of our domain, studies show that we are **much more influenced by situational factors** than we would like to believe.

Our readiness to go along with the crowd, to obey authority, to respond impulsively is a truth about human nature that some would prefer to discount. Yet, intuitively we know this is true. Why else would parents be wary when their kids start hanging out with the wrong crowd? Or a spouse gets too chummy with a friend of the opposite sex?

Studies show that situational factors often entice us to act differently from the way we usually act. They also indicate that we're poor judges of our own propensity to stray from our ideals, believing that we act better than we actually do.

Not that you know what is called a "fundamental attribution error", in the name of fairness, wouldn't it be a good idea to judge another's lapse of judgment at least as kindly as you judge your own?

Good Decision Making

With so many choices available to us today, being skilled at making good decisions is essential. So much so that *how* you make a decision is often more important than *what* decision you make.

Not knowing how to make a decision can cost you peace of mind both before and after the decision making process. Remember the many times you've second guessed your choice? Had buyer's remorse? Spent hours in your head trying to "undo" the choice you made?

You probably know that it's a good idea to weigh the pros and cons of a decision beforehand. But what else might assist you in making good decisions? Here are a few ideas that might be helpful:

Most good decisions involve a certain degree of risk.
Don't let the fact that there are risks involved in a choice unduly influence your decision. Instead, assess the risks and see if you can live with what might happen if things don't work out as expected. As Jawaharlal Nehru said, *"The policy of being too cautious is the greatest risk of all."*

Accept that you can't have it all.
Decisions force us to close the door on other possibilities – paths not taken, careers not chosen, experiences you didn't have. Would your marriage to your old love have worked out better? Fantasize all you like, but you'll never really know. So, visit the "what if" scenario if you must, but do not invite it to take up valuable real estate in your brain. Let the past be. Live in the present where good decisions can truly enhance your life.

Because a decision didn't work out as expected doesn't necessarily make it a bad decision.
If you decide to take a vacation in Florida in February and the weather is rainy, *c'est la vie*. This is not a bad decision, just one that didn't work out well. However, if you choose to spend your vacation in the Cayman Islands in the midst of hurricane season, this is analogous to an unforced error. Seek out the information you need beforehand so that the chances of your decision working out well are in your favor.

More thinking is not always better thinking.
Think. But if you tend to overdo the researching, ruminating and information seeking, stop. All analyses reach a point of diminishing returns. Good decisions can take place relatively quickly, based on intuition and quick thought, without painstaking assessment of endless data.

> **All analyses reach a point of diminishing returns.**

Don't defer decisions endlessly.
Sure there's a time to put off making a decision. Perhaps, you need more information. Or wish to consult with an adviser. Or wait for a less busy time. Just don't wait so long that the decision is made for you by circumstances or by others. Or, that you get so disgusted with your indecisiveness that you end up making an impulsive decision just to get it over with.

Improve your intuition.
Some people make great decisions by trusting their intuition. In contrast, others constantly get into trouble by "following their hunches". What's the difference? A well developed intuition is not just feeling lucky or acting impulsively. It consists of noticing nuances, observing details, assessing body language, awareness of tone of voice and more. These factors are important sources of information that help in making wise decisions.

It's Not Just This Or That

Too often we think in binary terms, giving ourselves a choice of two. It's this or that; take it or leave it; right or wrong; good or bad; smart or stupid.

It's natural to be tempted to think this way despite the fact that this mode of thinking has real impediments, particularly when dealing with human affairs. Consider these limitations:

If you don't fit into the "good" category, the only other place for you is the "bad" category. If you're not smart, you must be stupid. If you're not strong, you're weak. If you didn't make the right choice, you made the wrong one. No wonder people seek perfection. It's better to be in heaven than hell!

Thinking in binary terms implies a fixed, unmoving, static view of reality. On some rare occasions, that's appropriate. We can generally describe a child as a boy or girl. But smart or stupid, anxious or calm - sorry, it's just too simplistic a way of thinking.

Consider this real-life problem created by binary thinking:

> Jack believes he's dumb. Why? Everyone knows that his brother Ted is the "smart one" in the family. The bumper sticker that tells the world, *"My child is an honor student"* is not there because of Jack's achievements. Neither is the framed science award that hangs on the den wall. In this family, where binary thinking dominates, since Jack is not smart, he's stupid.

Jack's actually an average student. But average is embarrassing; mediocrity a disgrace. Grade point average is the only measuring device and Jack just doesn't make it. Never mind that he's a whiz at computer games. Or has a great sense of humor. Or enjoys playing the guitar. In his family, these skills are viewed as a waste of time, taking away from what's really important.

Binary thinking leaves no room for variations, gradations, nuances or desire. It ignores contradictions, meaning that a smart person can do pretty dumb things and vice versa. Clearly, we need a better way to think.

> **"A smart person can do pretty dumb things."**

I'd like to suggest an alternative, called **thinking on a continuum**. Let me give you an example of how this works.

Pick a trait that you can measure yourself on. For this exercise, let's use the level of anxiety that you typically experience.

Take a piece of paper and draw a horizontal line across the page, with the numbers "1" through "10" evenly spaced along the line. Rate your general anxiety level by putting an x on one of the numbers; the higher the number, the higher the anxiety. Let's say you rated yourself a "7".

Now, reflect on a situation that was challenging for you. Perhaps you were taking an important exam or undergoing an invasive medical procedure. Rate your anxiety level at that time. A typical response: *"Off the charts, a 12."*

Consider how your anxiety level might have changed if you treated yourself to a massage before the event. If you love massages, you might respond, *"At least for the moment, my anxiety zipped down to a 2"*. On the other hand, if you're squeamish about massages, your anxiety level might be raised by such a suggestion.

As you can see, thinking on a continuum is dynamic, not static. Rather than just thinking of yourself as an anxious person, you take into account situational factors, context, expectations, likes and dislikes. This richer, truer, more compassionate way of thinking helps you monitor your progress rather than relying on an external source as your standard.

So, next time you're thinking about how you rate, change your binary thinking (it's this or that) to thinking on a continuum. Getting used to thinking this way is a finer way to live, don't you think?

Thinking That Makes Things Worse

All thinking is not created equal. Indeed, some thinking actually impedes your ability to make good decisions or take effective action.

Here are typical examples of such thinking:

All or Nothing Thinking: It's black or white, no gray allowed.
"I have no other choice. I must do it this way."
"If I can't do it perfectly, why even try?"

Over generalizing: Using the words "never" and "always".
"This *always* happens to me."
"I can *never* count on you for anything. "

Exaggerating Responsibility: Shouldering too much of the blame.
"It's all my fault."
"Why didn't I know this was going to happen?"

Catastrophizing: Expecting the worst; treating disappointments as disasters.
"Nobody will ever want to be my friend."
"It'll be a disaster if I don't get this job."

Undermining Self: Being unappreciative of your coping skills.
"I don't know how I'll ever get through this."
"I was just lucky to pass the test."

Mind Reading: Being certain without corroborating evidence.
"She said my work was good, but she just wants to be nice."
"After what I did, I know everyone's going to hate me."

"If Only" Thinking: Believing that if one facet of life of your life were different, everything would be A-OK.
"I'd be happy *if only* my kids would behave."
"I'd be rich *if only* I had chosen a different career."

If you often think in these kinds of ways, it's time to make a change. *"The greatest discovery,"* wrote William James *"is that a human being can alter his life by altering his attitudes of mind."*

How to do this?

First step is to stay calm, for high intensity emotions and effective thinking are not a good combination.

Then define what the problem is, as focusing on the wrong question will

> **Focusing on the wrong question will never get you the right answer.**

never get you the right answer. Keep the problem in perspective, neither exaggerating nor minimizing the situation.

Differentiate good thinking from obsessing. Thinking gets you from point A to point B. Obsessing keeps you going round in circles so that your chances of coming up with a creative idea to solve your problem is practically non-existent.

If you find yourself obsessing about a problem, let go. The old adage of "sleeping on it" to gain a fresh perspective is wise. Return to the problem only when you are not so agitated and your mind is open to new ideas.

Once you are thinking with a clear mind, review the facts. Respect your emotions, but don't let them dictate your decisions. Examine the options. Consult with someone whose opinion you respect. Then decide what action, if any, you want to take.

Gaining Peace of Mind

Consciousness carries a price. As we become more aware and more mindful of 'what is', the precious commodity of peace of mind is often lost.

> **"Consciousness, rather than being a gift, can begin to feel like a curse."**

Our mind, which is our most important tool for survival, is designed to help us cope with our environment. Yet, in this age of global communication in which we're continually confronted with disturbing information about which we can do nothing, more knowledge may only mean increased agitation, anguish and confusion.

Consciousness, rather than being a gift, can then begin to feel like a curse.

Here's some advice for those of you who are longing for the peace of mind of an earlier time.

Cultivate Patience. This is one of the hardest habits to develop since we are so attuned to always *doing* something right away to make things better or safer. To cultivate patience, begin by acknowledging that you don't have control over many of the situations that you'd like to control. Respect that people have their own natures; events have their own timing. When faced with a stressful situation in which there's nothing that you can do, take a deep breath, relax and remind yourself that most upsetting events are not life-and-death matters. More likely, they simply do not fit into our preconceived ideas of how things should be.

Stop Orchestrating Other People's Lives. Be involved, be caring, be concerned. But don't micromanage or orchestrate another's life – not even your own children's once they are of a certain age. To be able to do this, you must develop a trusting mind, which is not synonymous with being naïve or stupid. Rather, it's dealing with life optimistically and enthusiastically, trusting that most experiences work out well. And for those that don't, trusting that you'll be able to cope or learn to cope with whatever happened.

Appreciate How Good Things Really Are. In the introduction to my book **Master Your Fears,** I wrote, *"It's strange that we live in an age in which we're healthier, safer, richer and living far longer than previous generations ever dreamed of, yet none of that makes us feel safer. Indeed, it's often true that the more we know, the longer we live, the wealthier we are, the more frightened we feel. Remember the days before seat belts, air bags, and bicycle helmets? Remember the days before we thought every lump and bump could be cancer? In those days we were actually more vulnerable, yet less aware of our vulnerability. We enjoyed life more because we knew less. Now, I'm not suggesting that ignorance is bliss. Or that we could possibly go backwards in time. But I am suggesting that we need to learn new ways to live an aware life with more courage and less fear."*

In our quest for certainty and safety, we often lose focus of the fact that peace of mind is not dependent upon absolute safety.

It's easy for our brains to go on overload with excessive exposure to what's going on in the world. Yet, there is no changing our new reality. It's our job to be able to filter out the noise, quiet our minds, still our scares and get on with our lives.

Telling Yourself Enough Is Enough!

It's a lucky kid whose parents know when to say "enough is enough". By doing so, parents help their kids move on.

Enough bickering with your brother!
Enough obsessing about that test!
Enough ruminating – make a decision already!

When parents say "enough is enough", they teach their kids that there is a time to make up your mind, let go, and move on. Too bad nobody does the same thing for adults. Many an adult is in desperate need of a caring party to tell him or her:

Make a Decision Already.
If you can't make up your mind because you're stuck in the "paralysis of analysis", stop before you hit the point of diminishing returns. After awhile, more analysis only 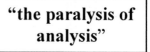 creates more confusion and adds nothing productive to your decision. Enough is enough!

Enough Arguing with Your Spouse.
After a certain point, does it matter who started it? Who's right, who's wrong? After you've said what you have to say, suppress the urge to repeat it again. There's a time to let go and create closure. Enough is enough!

Enough "Gloom and Doom".
Sure, you can feel bad about sad events, but there's a time to let go of your "gloom and doom". Don't keep

obsessing about all the terrible happenings in this world. Change the channel before the next murder story is aired. Turn the page before you get immersed in a new health scare alert. Limit the time spent with pessimistic, bad news people. Enough is enough!

Since generally no one is telling adults that "enough is enough", we must do this for ourselves. After all, if you keep holding on to yesterday's baggage and keep obsessing about distressing news, how will you ever have enough energy and enthusiasm to take on a new day?

The Damaging Duo – Stress and Worry

The art of living stress free is relatively simple in principle yet terribly difficult to put into practice. Nevertheless, if you can make progress in this endeavor, the results will be well worth the effort. Here's how to begin:

Reduce your worrying habit.
Who among us doesn't worry about the unknown from time to time – wondering whether a disaster will befall us, a loss will devastate us, a mistake will embarrass us, or, a "what if" tragedy will ruin everything? Some people, however, carry such worrying to an extreme. They worry too frequently, too intensely, too automatically - until worrying becomes their way of life. If you are one of these people, you must make a conscious effort to reduce your worrying ways.

Be concerned, not worried.
If your mind automatically veers toward worrying about all the things that could possibly go wrong, try transforming your worry into concern. Here's the difference between the two. With concern, you have a heightened awareness about a specific situation. If warranted, you take appropriate action, and then relax once the problem is dealt with. Worry, in contrast, can (and often does) continue non-stop. The worry may be about events that will never take place, inconsequential stuff, other people's issues or matters that you can do nothing about. Such worry drains your energy and hinders your ability to take action when necessary.

Worried or excited?
There's a thin line between feeling nervous and feeling excited. Worriers tend to lean toward the nervous side. Reverse this pattern by shifting your focus to what's exciting about a matter. For instance, if you're meeting a new person, rather than worrying about what she'll think of you, focus on the excitement that might arise from the interaction.

Recognize that there are few things in life that truly matter.
Many adults give great advice to their kids when they tell them that what's stressing them out will have little, if any, impact in the long run. As adults, we can appreciate that losing a playoff game, receiving an unfair grade, being teased by other kids are significant disappointments. Still, with life experience under our belts, adults know that such letdowns will not matter much, if at all, in the long run.

Great! But how smart are we adults with our own difficult moments? Do you remind yourself to keep things in perspective when you're stuck in traffic? Or your washing machine breaks down? Or a task took longer to do than expected? Or your spouse hasn't called? Or, do you get worked up at these moments, creating major stress - to no avail.

A caveat: I'm not suggesting that nothing matters. It's just that too often we put excess importance on events that are insignificant beyond the moment. One way to determine how important a matter might be is to reflect on whether it will have any significance 3 months from now.

Life is not about having it all or getting it all done.
Many adults rush through their lives at a frantic pace, trying to have it all. If you are one of these people, you

probably get up early, stay up late, have plans for every weekend, then wonder why you're so stressed. Add on a propensity for being dissatisfied with what you have and envying those who are richer, prettier, smarter, or stronger than you, is there any wonder that your life feels so pressurized? Life is not a race in which you have to come in first. More is not always better. Quantity is no substitute for quality. What is truly significant in life is how you experience the journey, not what you have in the end.

Avoid mentally making a catastrophe about future events.
Stressed people are inclined to dwell on the dreaded possibilities of "what might happen". They obsess about the worst case scenario, skipping past other more likely outcomes. Guard against your tendency to *overestimate* horrendous consequences while *underestimating* your ability to cope with whatever may happen.

Answer "what if" questions.
Worriers frequently ask *"what if?"* questions to dramatize and justify their worrying. *"What if* I get lost?" *"What if* she leaves me?" *"What if* I panic?" It's a problem when these questions remain unanswered. The solution: Answer the questions. Think about possible solutions such as - "I'll take a map with me," "I'll grieve, but I'll get on with my life," or "I'll excuse myself by saying I'm not feeling well." Planning coping strategies to resolve your worries is far better than letting worries fester inside your head.

Break down big problems into smaller, less threatening ones.
How can I stop drinking might be better dealt with as, "How can I become motivated to attend AA meetings?" How can I cope with a diagnosis of cancer might be

better dealt with as, "How can I find the best oncologist?" Accomplishing these smaller tasks will then empower you to face the bigger ones.

Limit the time you spend with pessimistic, doom and gloom people.
Sure they may be your friends, as "birds of a feather flock together". But such people are bad

> **"These people are bad for your emotional health."**

for your emotional health. Spend more time with optimistic, resilient people whose confidence rubs off on you.

Watch your language!
No, I'm not talking about curse words, I mean scare words. *"This is a catastrophe!"; "I'm scared to death!"; "Oh my God!"; "I'll never recover!"* If you've been magnifying your fear with such trigger words, stop. You don't need to turn every setback into a potential disaster or tragedy. Try using calmer talk such as, *"This is a big setback for me, but I will find a way to get past it."* Or, *"This is a tough situation; I need to talk to someone who can help."*

Place less importance on what other people think.
You have no control over what others think of you or what they are saying about you. Sure you can try to correct any misperception, but don't keep living your life around trying to please others - especially those who are so rigid in their ways that they will not change no matter what you do.

> **"Dwelling on the negative simply contributes to its power."**
> **Shirley MacLaine**

Taming Your Anger

In the past 6 months, how often have you felt steaming mad? How frequently have you gotten bent out of shape? How quickly did your annoyance beget anger, your anger beget rage? If your answer is *"never"*, you're a saint and can stop reading this column right now.

All others, read on.

If you know you need to control your anger instead of letting your anger control you, here's some advice to heed.

Be quick to recognize when you're getting angry so that you can tame your anger in its early stages.
Once the emotional part of your brain takes over, the rational part of your brain will be hard pressed to do anything effective to tame your anger. Hence, as soon as you begin to feel tense, take 3 deep breaths, relax your body, and say something reassuring to yourself, such as, "It's going to be okay." or "I can deal with this."

Examine your assumptions.
If you think that somebody is demeaning you or trying to put something over on you, anger will be a natural response. Examine your assumptions to see if there might be an alternative explanation for a behavior. For instance, if an associate keeps you waiting, does that mean he's demeaning you or that he's forgetful, overwhelmed or disorganized? Why not go with the less offensive assumption first and only move on from there if time proves you wrong.

Respond in ways that lower your anger level:
Accepting - "It's okay, at least for now."
Flexibility - "I'll think about it."
Understanding - "She has a lot on her mind these days."
Moderation - "I know it doesn't have to be perfect."

Avoid responding in ways that raise your anger level:
Righteous indignation - "How dare she?"
False sense of entitlement - "I shouldn't have to wait."
Perfectionism- "It's not the way it should be!"
Envy - "Why should he have more than I have?"

Though taming your anger is not easy to do, once you accomplish this skill, you will rejoice in the results.

Imagine not having to live with that knot in your stomach.
Imagine being able to relax and sleep well.
Imagine living your days with positive energy.
Imagine working cooperatively with others.
Imagine asserting a healthy sense of self without being overly aggressive.

For more ideas on how to tame your angry thoughts and behavior, check out the wise and witty book, **Taming Your Inner Brat,** by Dr. Pauline Wallin at www.DrWallin.com

---

> **"People are not prisoners of fate, but only prisoners of their own minds."**
> *Franklin D. Roosevelt*

The Nature of Happiness

The right to pursue happiness was so significant to our founding fathers that they made it one of our inalienable rights, guaranteed by the Declaration of Independence.

The Dalai Lama, spiritual leader of Tibet, proclaimed that "the very purpose of our life is to seek happiness." His book, "The Art Of Happiness" was a New York Times bestseller.

Many modern American parents devote an abundance of their time, money and energy to making their children happy. Much to their chagrin, their kids are often unhappy, dissatisfied with what they have and who they are.

With so much emphasis on happiness, one might think we should have learned by now how to be happy. Yet, for many, happiness remains an elusive and ephemeral goal.

Many pin their hopes for happiness on getting what they want. It could be a tangible item, such as a dream house or a snazzy sports car. Or it might be a great experience, such as a trip around the world or a fabulous party.

Some focus on relationships, thinking happiness would be theirs if only their kids would behave or their spouse would change. And still others hone in on a conceptual idea, such as success, popularity or a life of leisure.

If you are over the age of 10, however, you know that the thrill of something new just doesn't last. We tend to adapt quickly to what we already have and soon no longer feel that it's anything special. Then we look for more. People can spend their lives working at jobs they hate to buy things they think will make them happy, only to discover that their happiness quickly wanes.

To end this state of affairs, we need to gain a deeper understanding of the nature of happiness.

Studies show that people are happy not because they have a lot, but because they are happy with what they have. While happy people tend to experience what happens to them as good, unhappy people tend to zero in on whatever goes wrong.

As proof of this, don't you know people with lots of money who are constantly grumbling about one thing or another? And don't you know others who are of moderate means who are happy and satisfied with their lot in life?

Here are some quotes on the subject of happiness that I believe will enrich your understanding of the subject.

We act as though comfort and luxury were the chief requirements of life, when all that we need to make us happy is something to be enthusiastic about.
Charles Kingsley

Happiness is nothing more than good health and a bad memory.
Albert Schweitzer

If only we'd stop trying to be happy, we'd have a pretty good time.
Edith Wharton

Unbroken happiness is a bore; it should have its ups and downs.
Moliere

NOW I GET IT!

Happiness consists more in small conveniences or pleasures that occur every day than in great pieces of good fortune that happen but seldom to a man in the course of his life.

Benjamin Franklin

Happiness is as a butterfly which, when pursued, is always beyond our grasp, but which if you will sit down quietly, may alight upon you.

Nathaniel Hawthorne

The greatest part of our happiness depends on our dispositions, not our circumstances.

Martha Washington

Happiness is best defined as the difference between our talents and our expectations.

Edward De Bono

Happiness is not in the mere possession of money; it lies in the joy of achievement, in the thrill of creative effort.

Franklin D. Roosevelt

When one door of happiness closes, another opens; but often we look so long at the closed door that we do not see the one which has been opened for us.

Helen Keller

There are as many nights as days, and the one is just as long as the other in the year's course. Even a happy life cannot be without a measure of darkness and the word 'happy' would lose its meaning if it were not balanced by sadness.

Carl Jung

To be without some of the things you want is an indispensable part of happiness.

Bertrand Russell

Happiness is someone to love, something to do, and something to hope for.
Chinese Proverb

It's pretty hard to tell what does bring happiness. Poverty and wealth have both failed.
Ken Hubbard

And last, but certainly not least:

Happiness is a warm puppy.
Charles Schulz

It's Not Always Nice to be Nice

Do you pride yourself on being agreeable, considerate, thoughtful and nice? Do you view yourself as easy to get along with, sensitive to the needs of others, kind and conscientious? Do you strive to always do the "right thing"? These are admirable qualities. But, watch out, for being nice has its downside.

Be honest. Are there times you're disappointed when others do not reciprocate in kind? Do you often feel unappreciated, at times even exploited? Have your good feelings morphed into nasty feelings when you went out of your way to please another and it wasn't appreciated - or even noticed?

> **"We teach people how to treat us."**

By our actions, we teach people how to treat us. If you have taught others that it's okay for them to ignore your needs or that you put more importance on pleasing others than on pleasing yourself, expect some unpleasant fallout. Here are a few of the ways being nice can become not so nice.

Feeling That You're Being Taken Advantage Of.

- If you hate confrontation and are intimidated by negotiation, you may feel that the only option left is to give in and accommodate other people's wishes. This will inevitably backfire on you as you begin to feel that others are taking advantage of your good nature. Hence, reflect on alternative options before simply yielding to another's wishes. Even if you feel guilty about not pleasing another, a little guilt is far preferable to becoming embittered because your efforts weren't noticed or appreciated.

Resenting All That You Do.
- If you often feel frazzled by work, overburdened by responsibilities and resentful that you have no time to do your own thing, perhaps you're being too nice. Avoid the inclination to solve other people's problems. Guard against taking over responsibilities that are not your own. Don't always say "yes" to helping out. Saying "no" at times will actually make others more appreciative when you do say "yes". Setting reasonable limits on the time and energy you give to others has many satisfying long term benefits.

Apologizing Profusely.
- If you're usually the first one to jump in and apologize – not once, but repetitively - you may be trying too hard to be nice. If you do feel an apology is in order, communicate what you're sorry for, but avoid putting yourself down. Make your apology simple, direct and honest. Then move on to other topics.

A reminder:

Though it's good to be aware of the pitfalls of being nice, being nice is certainly an admirable trait. Indeed, the world needs more nice people. So, do not alter your basic tendency to be nice, agreeable and thoughtful. Just modify your inclination to undervalue yourself, give in too quickly and do things for others at your own expense.

Guilty About Feeling Guilty

Guilt is not necessarily a bad thing. It keeps us from behaving badly. It makes sure our malicious impulses don't get the upper hand. And if at times they do, guilt prompts us to make appropriate amends.

But as with everything else in life, guilt can be overdone.

> *"I always feel guilty about something. It could be what I've done, what I haven't done, or what I should've done,"* bemoans Lisa. *"It sounds crazy but I even feel guilty about feeling guilty. Help!"*

Lisa is not alone with her over-the-top guilt syndrome. Though such excessive guilt can affect anyone, it does tend to occur more frequently with women.

For some, guilt orbits around combining work and parenting.

> Beth explains, *"When I'm at work, I feel guilty that I'm not with my kids. And when I'm with my kids, I feel guilty that I'm not working. My husband, however, is so different. He feels zero guilt about going to work and leaving the kids. And when he's home, he doesn't feel guilty about work that still needs to be done. I wish life could be that simple for me."*

For others, guilt is their constant companion.

> Meet Dara, a devoted stay-at-home mom, who confesses that she's always feeling guilty about something. *"I'm with my kids a lot. I want to give them the best of everything. But*

I feel guilty that I don't discipline them enough. It bothers me that they are spoiled kids - selfish and unappreciative. I feel guilty that I created this monster, but I just can't seem to say no to them."

If your guilt seems to be more neurotic than healthy, what can you do to change the pattern? Here are some ideas:

Lower Those Impossibly High Expectations.
Guilt feeds on perfectionism. Lowering those over-the-top expectations is not synonymous with rewarding mediocrity. It's simply accepting that you're not perfect, you make mistakes, you don't always do your best, and situations don't always work out as well as expected.

Get Rid of the Approval Trap.
Stop trying so hard to make others happy. No matter how much effort you employ, some people will still complain and criticize. It doesn't mean you need to feel guilty about what you did or didn't do. As a kid, you probably thought that when your parents were upset, you had done something wrong. Only through the magic of maturity can you finally appreciate that their response had more to do with them than with you.

> **"...your parents' response had more to do with them than with you."**

Don't Take Yourself So Seriously.
Lighten up! If you make a mistake, don't turn it into a tragedy. If you forgot to do something, don't define it as a disaster. Responsible, reliable people still make goofs and gaffes. Indeed, as long as you live, you will continue to make faux pas. So, keep them in perspective. And never, ever lose your sense of humor.

NOW I GET IT!

If your guilt is still giving you a hard time, speak to it like it's an out-of-control adolescent. Demand that it chill out. Inform it that you no longer have need of a tyrant constantly monitoring your every move.

Then remind yourself of all the things you do right. Promise yourself that you will hold on to your healthy sense of guilt, but that your neurotic sense of guilt absolutely has to go!

Before and After

There's before and then there's after.

One day life is going on as it always has. The next day, life deals you such a blow that nothing will ever be the same.
"It can't be! How could this have happened? Wake me from
this awful nightmare and tell me it was all a dream."

But nobody does.

And nothing, absolutely nothing stops the ache in your heart. Nothing soothes the pain. Nothing makes the sadness go away. Nothing matters anymore.

You never had any warning, not even a hint of what the future would bring. How can you possibly deal with the loss? Your mind can't wrap itself around it. And when it does, so what? Your soul is in shock.

Just yesterday, everything was different. But that was before. And this is after. You're exhausted. You're depressed. No, depression is for people with a gray cloud over their heads. This is beyond depression; this is despair.

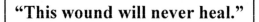 **"This wound will never heal."** People say time heals all wounds. They are wrong. This wound will never heal; nor should it. It would be sacrilegious to do so.

As time passes, you notice that each day is not the same. One moment, emptiness reigns, then loneliness. The next day, it's fear, then fury. One day, the melancholy is so deep that you don't know how you will ever go on. Yet you do.

You may want to be with friends or hide from them. You may want to sleep your days away or keep busy. You may have no interest in food or you may be thankful for a good meal. You may want all the painkillers you can get your hands on or you may experience a strange comfort in the pain.

There is no proper path; there is no right way; there is no one to guide you through the minefield.

Just know that no matter what you are feeling, you have the right to feel it. No matter what you are thinking, you have the right to think it. Take all the time you need to find a way to survive your After.

People's hearts and prayers are with you. They wish they could do something to ease your pain. They know they can't. But still they are there.

May you take a bit of comfort in their love and support.

What's Stopping You?

What are your favorite "don'ts" that stop you from doing what you need to do to be successful or happy? Perhaps you believe you don't have the talent, the money, the confidence, the know-how, the energy, the time, the looks, the brains, the motivation, the willpower.

Ten big don'ts! And there are many more. Hence, if I neglected to mention your dearest don't, add it to the list now.

What do these don'ts stop you from doing?

> *"I don't know,"* shrugged Jeff.
> *"I have no idea what I want,"* whined Winona.

If you, like Jeff or Winona, don't know what you want, how are you ever going to get it? Don't tell me you still believe in Santa Claus bringing you what you want. And by the way, how would he know what you want if *you* don't even know?

Marilyn Monroe once said, *"I wasn't the prettiest. I wasn't the most talented. I simply wanted it more than anyone else."* Obviously, there was a lot about Marilyn's life that didn't work, but if you're open to learning then know that anyone in life can be your inspiration.

If your *don'ts* and your *can'ts* are stopping you from getting what you want in life, here's some advice for you.

Do what interests you, even when there's more pain than gain.
When I first began skiing, I loved the sport—despite falling on almost every turn. Black and blue bruises be damned, this was too much fun to give up!

Learn to tolerate feelings of inadequacy.
There are days when you will feel incredibly dumb or klutzy. These are "bad days" - not a life position, unless you choose to make it so.

Quit comparing yourself to the best.
Sometimes people think they can't even *try* an activity (like writing or public speaking) because they won't be any good at it. They compare themselves to the best and fall short. Cut that out! No, you're not the best. You're not even average. You're just a beginner. Let yourself be one. Don't belittle what you're doing. Don't call yourself nasty names. And don't give credence to others' wisecracks.

Take an action.
Thinking, reading, talking, or wishing you could do something is often a good way to begin. But if you want to pursue an activity or reach a goal, you must take the plunge and do it. Thinking is no substitute for action.

If you still find yourself stuck and can't get moving to do what needs to be done, go back to your list of don'ts. Treat these don't as naughty children who are behaving badly. Give **Treat these don'ts as naughty children** them time-outs. Now that they are stuck in their room, you are free! Take the opportunity to go and do what you've always wanted to do. No excuses.

Do it now!

Doing What Doesn't Come Naturally

When you feel miserable, it's the most natural thing in the world to wallow in your misery.

Angry folks do it by obsessing about what others have done to them. Sad folks do it by recalling their hurts and disappointments. Worriers do it by anguishing about what bad things might happen.

Though there is something to be said for feeling miserable from time to time (how else would you appreciate the good?), many people hold on to negative emotions way too long. They don't just feel their emotions – they embrace them, defend them, indulge them – until these feelings get transformed into an identity.

The upshot: they no longer just feel angry, sad or worried; they become people with a chip on their shoulder, despair in their heart, fear in their soul.

If this is true for you, it's time for you to let go of your negative emotions by *doing what doesn't come naturally*. That is, you need to act contrary to the way you're feeling!

> **"Act contrary to the way you're feeling."**

If someone has gotten you so ticked off, you would like nothing more than to strangle him, it's okay to feel that way - for awhile. However if your anger is transforming you into a bitter, angry person, it's time to take an unnatural action. Though the last thing you might think of doing is something pleasant and nice, that is exactly what you must do. If you can't or don't want to be kindly to the one you're upset with, do something nice for yourself or for another deserving soul.

NOW I GET IT!

If you're down in the dumps, it's okay to feel that way - for awhile. However, if your sadness is transforming you into a depressed and joyless soul, it's time to take an unnatural action. Though your heart may not be in it, you must push yourself to do something that can lift your mood - listen to music, watch a movie, take a walk, play a game, do a task - any activity that gets you in touch with the lighter side of life.

If you're anxious about the future, it's okay to feel that way - for awhile. However, if your worries are transforming you into a nervous, apprehensive person, it's time to take an unnatural action. Despite the fear, you must face what needs to be faced, do what needs to be done. As William James said, *"We are afraid because we run away; we don't run away because we are afraid."*

Though it may seem counterintuitive to act contrary to the way you feel, that's often exactly what you need to do.

Supporters and Critics

When you make a difficult and controversial decision, you're likely to encounter those who support you and those who criticize you.

Supporters will listen with an open mind. They may be your #1 cheerleader or express more muted enthusiasm for your decision. No matter. You don't need everyone's total backing for everything you do. What supporters have in common is that they support you, even when they're not in total agreement with what you're doing.

Critics, in contrast, have firm ideas about how you should live your life. If you make a decision that's contrary to what they "know" is right, their response will either be a barrage of criticism, a look of disdain, or a deafening silence. Benevolent critics may wish you well but still undermine your confidence with their criticism. Malevolent critics will cut you off, humiliate or disparage you for your "stupid", "immoral", or "totally unacceptable" behavior.

If you want to treat yourself kindly, and I hope you do, always share your decision with your supporters before you tell your critics. And, even with supporters, give thought to how and when you share your news.

> **"Always share your decision with your supporters before you tell your critics."**

Your chances of receiving earnest support will increase if you present your decision as a well thought out conclusion rather than a spur of the moment impulse. Hence, if you decide to seek a divorce, come out of the closet, move out of the country or make a dramatic career change, those close to you will need to appreciate that you've given such life changing decisions serious thought.

Supporters, as well as benevolent critics, will likely have questions for you, especially if your news is taking them by surprise. Make the time and effort to answer their questions. Though you don't have to share everything, brushing off their questions as though they have no right to ask will not endear you to them.

Expect whoever you're telling to act 'in character'. Hence, if he thinks that homosexuality is a sin, expect him to feel that you're immoral when you announce that you're gay. If she thinks that those who initiate divorce are totally self-centered, expect her to focus on the pain you're causing rather than the pain you've been experiencing.

Though some critics never change, some do and may actually become your best support network. This is more likely to happen when:

- They've had time to adjust to your decision.
- The results turn out to be not as devastating as they feared.
- They don't want to lose their relationship with you.
- They become more understanding about why you made your decision.
- Society, in general, becomes more accepting of your chosen life style.

With those critics who continue to openly disapprove of you, it's best to keep an emotional distance. Don't be in their face with your new way of life but also don't be intimidated into silence or guilt. Though others don't have to embrace your life choices, they do need to respect who you are and what you're about.

Learning From Your Regrets

"If only I knew then what I know now." How often I hear that phrase replayed by those who dwell on missed opportunities and painful regrets.

Jane regrets dropping out of college to get married. "I wish I had a better education and made something of myself. Now that my kids are older, I'm bored. I would've liked to have an important career, but it's too late now," she laments.

Rick regrets taking the easy way out. "I entered my dad's business right after college. Financially, I've got no complaints. But I have a hard time shaking off the feeling that I would have become someone special if only I had had the courage to go out on my own back then."

Regrets like these can become a constant reminder of "what could have been". But it doesn't have to be that way. Regrets can also enlighten and be an incentive for new opportunity. Here's how that might happen:

> **Conquer your negative emotions.**
> People often imagine that they would have done things differently - if only they had known better. Yet, the decisive factor in their decision-making is often an emotional one, not a lack of information. Jane could still get her college degree, if she weren't afraid that the commitment would be too much for her. As she reflects on her past, she recognizes that feeling overwhelmed was the same reason she dropped out of school years ago. If Jane is to learn from her regrets, she needs to deal with her fears in a different manner this time.

Use your regrets to motivate yourself to take a different action.
Rick can motivate himself to do something different *now*, instead of simply regretting his long ago decision. Perhaps, he could move the business in a new direction, start a second career, or blaze a creative trail in a completely different field. Ruing your regrets is a passive approach to life; using your regrets to make a better life for yourself is a positive, active approach.

Anticipate future regrets before you make major decisions.
If Jane does decide to return to college, it would be helpful for her to anticipate what might make her regret *this* decision too. If her goal is to have a thriving career, she should choose an appropriate program. Simply taking the easiest courses (which would be her typical pattern) would likely result in her regretting her decision once again.

Use regrets to appreciate what's important to you now.
Rick imagines that he might have become a musician if he hadn't gone into his dad's business. But he conveniently ignores how music might play a role in his life now. Too often people assume that it's too late in life to make any changes. Not true, unless you get entrenched in the position that - it should have been a certain way then so there's nothing you can do about it now.

Many people regret decisions they've made or opportunities they've lost. But only a few make those 'woulda, coulda, shouldas' work for them.

> **Make your 'woulda, coulda, shouldas' work for you.**

You can be one of those people! It's never too late to use your regrets as a catalyst for revamping your life.

Dr. Linda Sapadin

Is Your Messiness Out Of Control?

"Someday I might need it!"

"You never know – it might come back in style."

"Don't touch my stuff!"

"I haven't finished the newspaper yet."

"I can't get rid of that. That's my senior prom dress!"

Let's face it. Many of us refuse to get rid of an awful lot of stuff - even when we admit that it would be better if we did. Instead, we amass piles. We collect junk. Our closets overflow. Our clutter embarrasses us. In short, our place is a mess.

> **"Many of us refuse to get rid of an awful lot of stuff."**

Sure, we think about getting more organized. But what do we do? Do we roll up our sleeves and finally get rid of our junk. Do we whittle our piles down to nothing? Do we organize our closets so that we can truly find what we want when we want it?

Some of us do.

Unfortunately, however, many of us do just the opposite. We keep those yellowing newspapers, as they may contain an item of interest. We hold on to those magazines, for one day we'll get around to reading them. No sense getting rid of those gift boxes; they're sure to come in handy one day. And so might those coupons, receipts and

52

other papers we hoard.

And what about those pants that are too tight? Don't give them away! Some day, for sure, you'll lose those 20 pounds! And those adorable baby clothes? How could anybody dispose of such precious items?

Even if you admit that you're a pack rat, you may be defending your cluttered lifestyle. After all, in our highly disposable society, isn't it a virtue to see treasure where others see trash? Why should it be a problem if you tend to hold on to what others let go of?

As with many behaviors in life, whether it's problematic or not, depends upon the degree. Mild clutter, a bit of a pack rat, limited accumulation is one thing. But once the mess gets beyond a certain point, it can become a serious emotional and relationship problem. Indeed, in the extreme, it can reach a point where no one can enter your home because stuff literally leaves no room for people.

If you believe that your messiness might be out of control, here are some questions to ask yourself. Do you:

- Compulsively acquire things by buying, saving, or getting free stuff?
- Defend your disorganization and clutter by insisting that's the way you must have it?
- Attach emotional significance to items that others view as junk?
- Have enormous anxiety about throwing things away?
- Organize stuff by visual or spatial cues rather than by categories? (For instance, keeping clothes on the floor where they're visible rather than putting them away in a closet.)

If after reading this column, you believe that you or (someone you love) has developed an amassing problem, do not ignore it or laugh it off. These traits tend to escalate, getting worse as time goes on.

Think of it this way:

A mess is okay. But a mess needs to be cleaned up if for no other reason than to make room for the next day's mess. A mess piled on top of another mess, piled on top of still another mess begets a life of turmoil, chaos and confusion.

When Your Need For Control
Is Out Of Control

You know the feeling: The urge to always do your absolute best, to ruminate about a decision until you drive yourself nuts, to insist that things must be done your way.

Perfectionism -
Obsessiveness -
Rigidity -
These are the components of the **Triple Whammy Syndrome.**

If this way of living describes you, you know how stressful life can be. When your need for control is out of control, this is what you must do:

Focus on the Basics.
The most basic need in life is to breathe. Take a few moments from your busy life right now to slow down. Take three deep breaths. Inhale s-l-o-w-l-y, exhale s-l-o-w-l-y. On the exhale, gently tell yourself, "It's okay to let go." Repeat two more times. If you've done this exercise (not just read it) you probably feel more relaxed already.

Accept What Is.
We, in the West, put so much emphasis on the importance of being in control that we don't even question this premise. In Eastern countries, however, the emphasis is on surrendering control; accepting what is. If you've got the triple whammy syndrome, you need to accept that many things are not in your control. This doesn't make it bad. You didn't do something

wrong. It's just how things are.

Delegate Control.
If you have a strong need for control, you will often feel overburdened and overstressed. Yet you hesitate to delegate control for you don't trust that the other person will do it the *right* way. Yet many tasks don't have to be done just one way or the best way. If you don't want everything to end up as your responsibility, let others do it their way – even if it's not done perfectly. Try it. You just might get used to enjoying less responsibility and more free time to spend as you wish.

Focus on what's Realistic, not Idealistic.
While, in the abstract, perfection may seem like a virtue, in real life it's most often a curse. If your need for control is so strong that the middle ground (what you call mediocrity) is unacceptable, don't be surprised if you're frequently disappointed. Change your goals so that you seek accomplishment, rather than perfection. There are lots of things in this world that need to get done, but do not need to get done perfectly (maintenance tasks, like cleaning and cooking are in this category). Still other tasks may not need to get done at all (re-doing what somebody else did because it's not perfect is in this category).

Accept Yourself with All Your Flaws.
We tend to treat others (particularly those close to us) the way we treat ourselves. Hence, one way to ease up

> **"We tend to treat others the way we treat ourselves."**

on your rigidity is to be kinder to yourself. Quick, list five things that are 'right' about you. Now, list five things that are 'wrong' with you. Which of these questions was easier for you to respond to? If your flaws are etched into the front of your brain while your virtues are tucked away in the far recesses of your gray matter, it's time to reverse your thinking. You don't have to be perfect to accept yourself as is.

Deliberately Do Something In A New Way.
Prove to yourself that you can be more flexible by changing how and when you do a task. Modify your daily routine. Take a new route to work. Say "yes" to a request you usually say "no" to. Make a deliberate mistake just to prove to yourself that mistakes aren't the end of the world. Most things turn out just fine. And if on occasion it doesn't, trust that you'll be able to adapt to what happens, becoming wiser as a result of your experience.

NOT ONLY A KID'S PROBLEM

It runs in families. It affects adults as well as kids, women as well as men, achievers as well as those who are embarrassed by their failures.

What is this culprit called Attention Deficit Disorder? Is there a test that determines whether you have it or not? And if you have it, can you do anything about it?

ADD is a neurobiological condition that affects how the brain and body work. Diagnosis is determined via symptom checklists, behavior rating scales, and a detailed history of past and current functioning.

The three major problem areas are: inattention, impulsivity and hyperactivity. When there is a hyperactive component, it is referred to as ADHD.

If you are wondering if you have ADD, here's a list of typical symptoms:

Inattention

-Inattentive to important details.

-Often making careless mistakes.

-Trouble organizing tasks.

-Difficulty screening out distracting stimuli.

-Trouble sustaining focus and concentration.

-Often losing and forgetting things.

Impulsivity

-Making impulsive decisions.

-Interrupting others in conversation.

-Intruding on other people's space.

-Getting upset with little provocation.

-Low frustration tolerance.

Hyperactivity

-Can't sit still, fidgets and squirms.

-Often feeling restless, has to keep moving.

-Difficulty with self-control.

-Can't enjoy quiet activities.

-Hard to stay with a task until completion.

If you're thinking, "who in this busy multitasking world doesn't have these symptoms", think again. As with almost all problems, it's not all or nothing - it's a matter of degree.

It's particularly helpful for adults who think they may have ADD to obtain a professional evaluation. If diagnosed with ADD, the next step is to plan a course of treatment with these elements:

Educational – Understanding your specific symptoms and knowing how they handicap your performance.

Coaching – Having a coach work with you to get organized and stay on track. It's best if a coach is not a family member, as coaching with family members tends to turn into nagging.

Creating Structure and Systems – Learning how to use lists, reminders, Post-it Notes, and filing systems.

Designing Reasonable Tasks – Learning to break big tasks down into small, achievable ones which reduces the anxiety associated with complex tasks.

Setting Deadlines – Creating your own personal deadlines to make you feel more in control.

Learning Compensatory Coping Skills – Developing ways to improve your memory, increase your ability to concentrate, manage your stress, calm your body, focus your mind and increase your frustration tolerance.

Using Technology Tools as an Aid – Learning how computer programs, PDA's and other technology can assist you in achieving your goals.

Psychotherapy and Support Groups – By the time most adults are diagnosed with ADD, they've lost confidence in their ability to achieve. Individual as well as group psychotherapy can provide important insights, useful feedback, support and encouragement.

Medication – While it's best not to view drugs as *the* answer, many find that medications are useful in helping one focus attention, increase motivation and ward off depression and anxiety.

If you do discover that you have ADD, you'll probably feel relieved that you're not lazy, crazy, dim-witted or just don't give a damn. Still, you do have a problem that needs to be addressed.

> **"You're not crazy, lazy, dim-witted or just don't give a damn."**

NOW I GET IT!

A young man, recently diagnosed with ADD expressed his relief this way:

> "I grew up wondering what was wrong with me. Everybody was always yelling at me to apply myself and try harder. But it never made any sense to me; I was doing the best I could.
>
> Finally, after all these years of feeling bad about myself and constantly disappointing others, I know what's wrong with me.
>
> Now for the first time ever, I've discovered a way to feel good about myself and achieve some success in this world."

Living on the Edge

His pattern was long standing. He was the kind of kid who got through school ignoring all assignments until the night before. That's when he'd pull an all-nighter and surprisingly ended up with rather decent grades.

His success re-enforced the pattern so that he began to take pride in his modus operandi of waiting to do things until he was under the gun. Much like Superman, he would lay low until the right moment, then summon up extraordinary powers of will, action, speed and endurance to achieve triumphant success.

> **"…waiting to do things until he was under the gun."**

Today he's a corporate attorney and openly admits that his crisis-maker style of putting things off has not always served him well. "It used to be exciting to wait until the last minute to get things done," he confessed. "My time was my own. I could do whatever I wanted until the last, critical moment. Then I would rush into action like a super-hero. For years, I relished the high drama that went along with living on the edge. Now, it's just plain exhausting."

He admitted that he was largely responsible for creating the last-minute crises that he weathered so well. Reflecting on this fact, he wondered how much pride he could genuinely take in calming the chaos he had caused. And how much longer could he continue to enjoy repeatedly risking disaster by letting calls, reports, filings and briefings wait until the last possible moment.

If this crisis-maker style of living feels familiar, here are some suggestions for modifying your ways:

Don't wait for an activity to lure you into action.
Rather than thinking, "An activity has to interest me before I can get involved in it," think "I have to be involved in an activity before it can interest me." This small change in attitude can make a big difference in action.

Rather than relying on stress or pressure as your primary motivator, develop a variety of reasons to start and finish an activity.
Other motivators might be: financial rewards, enhanced reputation, personal sense of accomplishment, less conflicted relationships, and pride in keeping your promises.

Don't let your momentary feelings dictate your actions.
Instead, focus on the consequences that would likely occur if you do not take timely action. And consider how you will feel about yourself if you fail to achieve your objective simply because you procrastinated on the matter.

Change a boring task into an interesting one by being creative.
Make a contest out of a dreary task. One way to accomplish this is to play the game "Beat the Clock". Create a challenge for yourself by setting a timer and seeing how quickly you can finish the job.

If you hesitate to change your pattern of 'living on the edge' because you fear life would be dull and boring without it, read the words of one reformed crisis-maker:

"My life today is sane. I feel so much better now that I'm not constantly in chaos. I get a lot accomplished. I've more energy to do what I want to do. People respect me. What could be bad?"

PART 2

COMMUNICATION COUNTS
We need to communicate well
so that the other person 'gets' us.

The limits of my language mean the limits of my world.

Ludwig Wittgenstein

...let us go down there and confound their language, that they may not understand one another's speech.

Genesis 11:7

Dr. Linda Sapadin

How to Respond to a Put-down

Wouldn't it be great if people went out of their way to appreciate what you did right instead of berating you for what you did wrong?

Wouldn't it be fantastic if people nixed their insults, squelched their criticisms and instead did nothing but support and encourage you?

Before you remind me how starry-eyed my fantasy is, let me enjoy my moment of reverie!

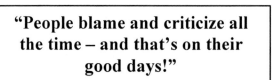

"People blame and criticize all the time – and that's on their good days!"

Okay, micro vacation over. Now I'm back to earth, ready to live in the real world where people blame and criticize all the time - and that's on their good days! When they really have an ax to grind, they add insults, curses, ridicule and humiliation. You, at some time, will be on the receiving end of such put-downs. How should you respond?

Most people are familiar with only four strategies:

- Respond defensively, explaining why the criticism is unfair.
- Respond defensively, justifying why you did what you did.
- Respond offensively, attacking the attacker.
- Say nothing and silently stew.

On occasion, these strategies are okay. Most often, however, they end up as attacks and counter attacks, laced with blame and shame. Thus,

66

it's a good idea to expand your repertoire of responses so that you have more creative, effective ways to respond when you are unfairly criticized.

Agree with what's been said, but disagree with the negative value judgment.
"Yes, I've been working slowly on this project, but that's okay. My aim is to create a quality product."

Respond to the process (what's happening) not to the content (the specific words uttered).
"I can see you're uptight today. Did something happen that I should know about?"

Agree that you did something wrong, apologize, but don't make it an earthshaking event.
"Yes, I should have called earlier to cancel. I'm sorry I didn't. I apologize. Let's see if we can make another date."

Disagree with the other person but try to understand his viewpoint.
"I don't think I did anything wrong, but I see you're upset. Tell me specifically what's upsetting you, so I can fully understand."

Enlighten the other person about your sensitivities.
"I feel demeaned when you speak to me with that tone of voice. You may think there's nothing wrong with it, but it feels patronizing to me."

Offer the person another way to phrase what he said.
"I don't mind if you call me 'sensitive'. It's the 'overly sensitive' that bothers me."

Say what's upsetting you succinctly. Often the less you say, the more powerful your message is.
"What you just said to me is totally unacceptable. You know I don't deserve to be treated that way."

If you've been unfairly put-down, your goal should be to respond with valuable and constructive information in a confident, strong (but not nasty) tone of voice.

Learning to Interrupt

Once they open their mouths, some folks don't know how to relinquish the floor. They seem unable to differentiate monologue from dialogue, dissertation from conversation, minutiae from significant details.

When you're part of such a "conversation", you may initially think of yourself as being a good listener. However, before long you will realize that you have become the captive audience for a person who will drone on for as long as you allow it to happen. Know that in these types of situations, you not only have a right to interrupt, you have an obligation to do so.

Here are a few tips on how to develop the skill of interrupting:

Interrupt by first using the person's name; then complete your sentence.
"Marge, I understand what you're saying; it's happened to me too."
"John, let's get to the bottom line here."

Interrupt with a statement about time.
"I only have another minute to chat."
"You've been talking about this for 20 minutes now; time to move on."

Interrupt by segueing into another topic.
"That's some story. But now I want to talk about something else."
"I need to interrupt you to tell you about what happened to me today."

Interrupt with honest feedback.
"I get the point of the story. Enough details."
"I haven't been able to get a word in edgewise. You've got to give me a chance to talk too."

Interrupt with an ending statement.
"I've gotta go. Talk to you another time."
"I'm already late for an appointment. Goodbye."

If you're someone who thinks you couldn't possibly implement any of these strategies, think again. None of these statements are rude, crude or attacking.

> **They are simply ways of holding your own when you are being held hostage.**

Your Words Matter

Often we have no realization of how significant our words are. Sometimes, this is good news, other times it's astoundingly bad.

First, the good news.

Kim received a greeting card from Nina, an old friend whom she hadn't been in touch with for many years. Her friend wrote:

> "Just want to let you know how often I think of you. Also, to express how grateful I am that you encouraged me to go back to school. I still remember the day you said, 'You can do anything you put your mind to.' Today, I'm celebrating my 5th anniversary as an elementary school teacher. I love making a difference in kids' lives. You were the catalyst that set me on the right track."

Though Kim treasured her friend's words, she was surprised that she had been so influential in her life. She had no memory of the conversation that Nina wrote about. Still, she knew from her own experience, that it wasn't so unusual for a friend's casual comment to have major significance in a person's life.

Now, here's the bad news.

Amy was seething. It was the second anniversary of her mother's death. So far, the day had passed without her husband, Rick, mentioning it. The evening was almost over when Amy exploded.

"You know how important my mother was - to both of us. How could you ignore the anniversary of her death? How come you don't speak about her any more?"

Rick felt ambushed by Amy's attack. He had not forgotten the day; indeed, he had been thinking about his mother-in-law a lot that day. She had been a great lady and he missed her. He was quiet for a moment. Then, he said,

"You told me you didn't want to talk about her. You told me it was too painful to even go there."

"I told you that?"

"Yes, you did."

"When?"

"Several weeks after she died. You said that you were hurting too much. That you had to stop talking about her and that you had to get on with your life."

"I don't remember saying that. If I did, it must have been an especially bad day for me. Did you think I meant I didn't *ever* want to talk about her?"

"I'm sorry, Amy. I don't know what I thought. But I do remember your pain when you said that and I didn't want to make you feel sad again. I also thought that if you wanted to talk about her, you would initiate the conversation."

Now it was Amy's turn to explain.

"Sometimes I say things that I mean, but then my feelings change. Maybe there was a time when I needed to stop talking about her. But I didn't mean that we should *never* talk about her. Check it out with me, if you're not sure about how I feel or what I want to do."

"I'm sorry."

"I'm sorry too. If I wanted to say something, I should have just done it and not waited for you to initiate the conversation."

Sometimes, the words etched in our brains are precisely what we should remember. Other times, those words are just what we need to let go of. If you are giving significance to what someone said a while ago, don't hesitate to inquire if the person still feels the same way today.

> **"People change and forget to tell one another."**
> **Lillian Hellman**

Dr. Linda Sapadin

How to Have That Tough Talk

"I know I need to tell her, but I don't know how."
"Facing it with him is just too hard for me to do."
"I don't have the courage to talk to him, so I avoid the topic."

It's not easy to:
-Confront a delicate matter.
-Raise a sensitive subject.
-Criticize one you love.
-End a relationship.
-Discuss end of life issues.

When people are uncomfortable talking about such difficult matters, they often avoid the topic rather than chance saying the

> **"Avoidance may only make things worse."**

wrong thing. Yet, avoidance may only make things worse. If you've been unable to have that tough talk, here are guidelines that will help you make such a conversation easier.

If you don't know how to start a tough talk, begin by saying just that.
Two examples: *"I don't know how to say this but I must tell you something."* Or, *"I don't want to scare you, but there's something you need to know."* It's possible, indeed probable, that you will be awkward as you speak. Hence, you might want to rehearse your first line. After that, however, be spontaneous. Say what you need to say - even though you're scared, embarrassed, or can't hold back the tears.

Address the issue without coming to the worst possible conclusion.
Beginnings set the stage for what comes next. Thus, begin your tough talk with a moderate statement, such as, *"I don't think you wanted to hurt me, but I was hurt when you didn't meet me at the doctor's office."* Don't start off with an extreme statement -*"You don't care about me."* Or the worst outcome -*"I could have dropped dead of a heart attack because you weren't there."*

Be charitable in your interpretation of the other person's behavior.
Sometimes tough talks are daunting because you're thinking such hostile thoughts that there's no way to say what's on your mind without it sounding dreadful. If this is true for you, creating a more generous interpretation of what happened will make the conversation easier. An example: You expected him to call. He didn't. Is he selfish and inconsiderate or so busy that it slipped his mind? Is his blunder a mistake, misdemeanor, felony or deserving of capital punishment? If you're so nervous about bringing up a subject, chances are you've intimidated yourself by your own negative interpretation.

Though sharing awful news is painful, avoiding the topic usually makes things worse.
It's heartbreaking when you must speak with someone about a serious illness, a need for a nursing home, an impending divorce. Though finding a better time to have the conversation may be a good idea, putting it off indefinitely is not the way to go. Continuing to avoid the topic creates unnecessary hurt and sometimes irreparable damage to significant relationships.

Dr. Linda Sapadin

Watching What You Say At Home

You have a choice. Every time you communicate something to your partner, your choice of words, your tone of voice and your body language can nurture or injure your relationship.

Andy took my statement as bad news.

> *"Are you suggesting that I should watch what I say when I'm at home? I can't be free to say whatever I think? You've got to be kidding."*

No, I'm not kidding! Though I don't mean to take it to the extreme, suggesting that you need to monitor your every word, I am telling you that **how you communicate matters. A lot!**

Let's look at an example:

> **She:** *Something's bothering you. What is it?*

> **He:** *Nothing's bothering me - I just want some peace and quiet. Is that too much to ask?*

> **She:** *There you go again; refusing to talk to me. What's the matter with you?*

> **He:** *The matter with me? The matter is you. You're always nagging me about something. Can't you ever shut up?*

> **She:** *Don't tell me to shut up. You're abusive. I've had it with you! We should get divorced.*

76

> **Batten down the hatches;**
> **you can see where this conversation is going!**

Now let's imagine that she starts off with the same remark, but because both parties communicate respectfully, they end up in a better place.

She: *Something's bothering you. What is it?*

He: *Nothing's bothering me! I just had a stressful day and want time to relax. Would you let me be?*

She: *Okay, but I can see there's something bothering you. When you're ready to talk to me about it, I'm here to listen.*

He: *I know, but sometimes I just like to be quiet. I'm not like you, always wanting to talk about things.*

She: *Yeah, I know you're a quiet kind of guy. It bugs me, but I guess it's better than a motor mouth guy. But it makes me feel so distant when you won't talk to me. You know you don't have to deal with everything by yourself.*

He: *I know you mean well, but right now, I'm zonked. We can talk later.*

She: *That's fine. But I need you to keep your promise.*

He: *I will.*

What did this couple do to make their communication work? How did they de-escalate the conflict? Here's what made the difference.

- *They acknowledged their different personality styles in an accepting manner.*

- *They stated their own needs without attacking their partner.*

- *They did not speak disdainfully about their partner's ways.*

- *They avoided gridlock by looking for a solution to the conflict.*

- *They created a temporary ending before one or both of them became enraged.*

- *At times, they used light words and a light tone of voice.*

- *They weren't afraid to back down from their original position.*

- *They didn't have an agenda to make the other wrong and themselves right.*

Communication counts. Relationships thrive or fail based upon what is said, how it's said and when it's said. And yes, this may mean monitoring what you say – even when you're in the comfort of your own home!

Authentic Apologies

I once knew a woman who said *"I'm sorry"* with such frequency that her friends kept telling her, *"enough with the apologies."* In contrast, I once knew a man (more than one, if truth be told) who would rather hang upside down by his toes than admit he was sorry.

Those who have an aversion to apologizing only do it when they're caught red-handed or have painted themselves into a corner. Under those circumstances, an *"I'm sorry"*

An aversion to apologizing...

is not a bona fide apology. Rather, it is a self-serving statement - a form of damage control that is designed to save one's skin. Such an apology neither indicates change of heart, nor responsibility for the pain that one has caused. In short, the person still doesn't 'get it'.

Here are examples of self-serving apologies:

- **Lacking understanding of the offense.**
  "If I've offended you, I'm sorry."

- **Evading responsibility for the hurt.**
  "I'm sorry you feel hurt but...."

- **Blaming the victim.**
  "You're too sensitive; where's your sense of humor?"

- **Seeking to create closure prematurely.**
  "I said I'm sorry; what else do you want?"

We often hear such self-serving statements from politicians and celebrities who issue public apologies. People don't take such apologies seriously because they are too little (no real concern for those they injured) and too late (apologies come *after* they're in so much hot water that their purpose is clearly damage control).

Too frequent apologies may also lack sincerity, as the remorse emanates from a need to self-disparage or to make nice rather than a real recognition of how one acted inappropriately.

Though there is no politically correct script to follow, there are three essential elements that will make an apology ring true.

- Acknowledgement of the hurt you've caused or the harm you've done.

- Recognition that you are in essence "begging the other person's pardon", not demanding that the apology get you off the hook.

- You are authentic in deed as well as in words. Apologies wear thin when the words seem genuine but the offending actions are repeated.

Authentic apologies can do much to heal wounds. Insincere apologies only add salt to the wounds.

Speaking So You're Taken Seriously

Laura sounded desperate.

> "Tommy's only 3 years old and he pays no attention to me when I speak to him. Maybe I'm just not cut out to be a mom. I don't know what to do. I've tried everything."

Before I could reply, there was a loud crash. Tommy had knocked over a basket of toys. Laura jumped up, apologized profusely and began picking up the toys. Tommy had an impish grin on his face.

> "Tommy, would you help me pick up the toys?" Laura pleaded. "Tommy, come help Mommy. I think it's time to pick up the toys now, okay?"

Tommy continued to scribble with the crayons.

> "Tommy, listen to Mommy, please?"

> "No, you pick up the toys. I'm making a picture."

When Laura finished cleaning up, she looked at me with tears in her eyes. Tommy ran over to her, showing her his drawing.

> "Mommy, don't cry. See, I made this picture for you."

Laura grabbed a tissue and gazed at Tommy.

"Sometimes he's so sweet. I hate it when I get upset with him. But I also hate that he has the upper hand. He knows how to get the best of me, don't you think?"

Laura had been struggling since childhood to get her parents to listen respectfully to her. Now her own little boy had joined the ranks, ignoring her when she spoke. Laura hated her parents' mocking statements such as, "Who do you think you are, miss smarty-pants?" Now, Tommy was starting to act in a similar manner.

Laura was determined to raise her child in a respectful manner, so that he grew up feeling strong and self-confident (not like her). Now she wondered if she was doing the right thing, for her little guy was running roughshod over her.

Must she change her ways and become her parents' clone, intimidating her child so that he would listen to her? She dreaded the thought. There had to be an alternative. And there was.

Here's what I told her:

"You need to learn to speak in a way that demonstrates that you're the one in charge. What you're doing is demonstrating weakness."

Laura was surprised when I told her that. She believed that her "nice" talk was showing Tommy that she was a caring and kind mommy. But Tommy was taking it to mean that she was a weak and powerless mommy, somebody who didn't have to be taken seriously.

Laura did not have to take a rough and gruff approach, as she feared. She did not have to ridicule Tommy or treat him harshly. She just needed to eliminate her weak speech patterns. Here are 5 ways her speech indicated weakness:

-**Using qualifiers**: *"I think, I guess, kind of, maybe."*

-**Putting a tag line at the end of a sentence**: *"It's time to pick up the toys, okay?"*

-**Asking a question instead of giving a command**: *"Would you pick up the toys?"* vs. *"Pick up the toys!"*

-**Pleading, excessive politeness**: *"Listen to Mommy, please?"*

-**Making self-disparaging remarks**: *"I'm not a good mother."*

Learning to speak with a stronger voice helped Laura develop greater authority and self-confidence. Though not a quick-fix miracle cure, Laura swears that at times it seems that way.

The last time I heard Laura talk to Tommy she said, "Tommy, time to go now." As he started to dawdle, she said, "Get your jacket on NOW!" As he obeyed, our eyes met. Nothing more had to be said. We both knew how far she had progressed with her wish to be taken seriously.

> **"Nobody can make you feel inferior without your consent."**
> *Eleanor Roosevelt*

One or Two Whines a Day, Max

> ## A small amount of whine can be good for your health.

After all, life can be exasperating and when you're frustrated, you need to find some way to let off steam.
> *"It's not fair!"*
> *"I was ripped off!"*
> *"She shouldn't have said that!"*

You whine a little. You tell your story to a few empathetic people. And voila, you feel better. Amazingly simple and effective therapy!

But habitual whining? Well that's a story of a different color. More than one or two whines a day are simply not good for your health. Indeed, it grates on other people's nerves, creates a victim mentality and holds you back from finding more mature ways of expressing yourself.

Most children learn early on in life that whining is an effective means to get what they want from their parents. Since whining is so annoying, parents tend to give in to it just to shut their kid up. By the time a child is approaching the teen years, however, habitual whining should be winding down.

Like many other childhood behaviors, whining becomes particularly unattractive the older you get. Whereas young children have few options to get what they want except by manipulating their parents, adults can and should understand that the world does not revolve around them, was not designed to satisfy their every desire and that they must develop more effective ways than whining to get their needs met.

If you can admit that your whining is out-of-control, here's what you must do to change the pattern:

- Instead of whining when something goes wrong, seek a solution to the problem.

- Instead of whining when you're disappointed, simply acknowledge your disappointment and then move on to plan B.

- Instead of whining about situations that you have no control over, focus on what you can do, given the circumstances.

- Instead of perpetuating that whiny, helpless, "I'm a victim" voice, practice putting forth a strong, self-confident voice that connotes competence and confidence.

Discipline yourself to one or two whines a day, max. Beyond that is simply not the way to go - unless you have a bizarre desire to make whining your pinnacle achievement.

The Runaway Inflation of Everyday Speech

Though Jason was reluctant to bring his new girl friend home, he finally consented to do so. Everything seemed to go well - until the next day.

"Mom, what did you think of Marla?"

"She seemed nice."

"Oh no, you hated her."

"What? I didn't say I hated her. I said she seemed nice."

"Only nice?"

"Yes, very nice."

"But you didn't think she was terrific?"

"I just met her. She was sweet and pleasant. She seemed nice. What's the matter with nice?"

"You're just saying that. I could tell you didn't like her."

"No, I like her. What did you want me to say, that she was amazing, astonishing, awesome?"

"She wasn't?"

"Jason, give me a break!"

"See, I told you, you didn't like her."

I don't know when perfectly respectable adjectives like *'nice'*, *'good'* and *'smart'* became 'not good enough'. Perhaps it happened when people began to go to elaborate lengths to emphasize the positive. That's when a smart kid became a *'genius'*, a pretty girl became *'drop dead gorgeous'* and a rich guy became a *'gazillionaire'*.

Perhaps word inflation simply follows the inflation that has occurred in other areas of society. When the majority of students at an Ivy League school receive an A in a course, then a B+ becomes a disappointment, a B pathetic. When high school students drive new BMW's to school, then a pre-owned Ford, even in good shape, is perceived as far less than adequate.

Sometimes this exposure to verbal inflation begins early in a child's life. For instance, if Johnny goes tinkle in the potty and mommy is *very, very* excited and daddy is *really, really* proud and grandma buys Johnny a *very special* present for the occasion, then superlatives become the norm and less ecstatic responses are viewed as deficient.

I think it's perfectly honorable for *"good"* to be good, *"nice"* to be nice, and *"fine"* to be fine.

> **Will you join me in my campaign to resist the runaway inflation of everyday speech?**

Discover Your *But*

Want to improve your communication skills? Want to zip up your energy level?

Well then, it's time for you to discover your *but.*

> Here's Jared's *but:*
> *"I'd love to play the guitar, **but** I'm so busy I can never find the time."*

> Here's Zoë's *but*:
> *"I'd love to quit my boring job, **but** I'm afraid I won't be able to find another one."*

This word *but* is tricky. It's a tiny little word that yields great power in our lives. Our job is to make this power work for us rather than against us.

Let's see how this works. What feelings are generated for you as you read these two sentence stems?

> *"You're doing a good job, **but**. . . ."*

> *"You're a nice guy, **but**. . . ."*

Were you feeling angst about what would follow the *but*? Were you anticipating bad news? If so, you're right on the money. A *but* sentence has two parts: one positive, the other negative. The essential message of such a sentence is what follows the *but*. What precedes it is just there to soften the blow or provide the excuse.

Hence if you want to defeat the negative influence of a *but* sentence, here's what you must do.

First Option: Place the *positive part* of your statement *after* the *but*. Doing so will help you become more action oriented. Notice the difference:

> *"I want to revise my resume by the end of the day, **but** I hate working on it."*

> *"I hate working on my resume, **but** I want to revise it by the end of the day."*

Can you feel the resistance in the first sentence? Can you sense the optimism in the second sentence? Ending on a more positive note helps fight the resistance!

Second Option: Replace the word *but* (which connotes resistance) with *and* (which connotes connection). Compare these sentences to Jared and Zoë's *but* sentences.

> *"I never seem to find the time, **and** still I'd love to play the guitar."*

> *"I want to quit my boring job, **and** I need to find a job before I can do so."*

Shifting from *but* to *and*, helps prevent resistance from overpowering desire. Also, giving both parts of the sentence equal significance practically implores you to take an action to create a resolution.

> *"I never seem to find the time, **and** still I'd love to play the guitar; Sunday evening is a good time to make it happen."*

> *"I want to quit my boring job, **and** I need to find a job before I can do that; I'll make it a priority to contact a headhunter to investigate new job opportunities."*

People typically speak with little awareness of how their word choices

> **"…word choices affect behavior."**

affect their behavior. Now that you know better, however, make it a point to use the word *but* to contribute to, rather than diminish, your power.

Getting Stuck On "Why?"

Most people believe that more communication means better communication. Time and again, this has proven not to be true. Increased communication may simply (though not always) make matters more distressful.

One example of this is the tendency to repetitively ask (either yourself or others) questions that begin with "Why?" or "How Come?"

Two examples:
>*"Why did I make such a stupid mistake?"*
>*"How come she doesn't visit me more often?"*

If you find yourself frequently asking these kinds of questions, stop! These are bogus questions. Though they masquerade as an honest wish to understand why, such questions are about as useful as a parent asking a kid *"How come your room is such a mess?"* In the history of civilization, how many parents do you think ever received a satisfying answer to that question?

> **"How come your room is such a mess?"**

Instead of torturing yourself with such useless questions, here's what you should be doing:

Make a statement about the situation.
Instead of those fruitless 'Why' questions, you might say, *"I wish I hadn't made that mistake,"* or *"If you can, I wish you would visit more often."* Or, your sentence might focus on putting forth a goal, such as: *"I'm determined not to make that kind of mistake again."* Notice that these are not blame statements, but

acknowledgments of feelings, thoughts or intended actions.

If you still feel the need to ask questions, begin your questions with "What" or "How".
For example, *"What can I do to earn more money so I can get out of debt?"* or *"How can you manage your time better so that you won't be late?"* These questions, unlike the "Why" and "How Come" ones, have meaty answers that can be quite valuable.

Why questions are not only unproductive, they are also detrimental to maintaining good relationships.
Think of how grateful your spouse will be if you quit saying, *"Why do you always leave the towel on the floor?"* or *"How come you're never on time?"* Though other peoples' habits may get on your nerves, it's better to express your annoyance with a statement or a proposed solution than to repeatedly ask questions that have no satisfying answer.

Instead of obsessively asking why, learn from your regrets.
"Why did this happen?" is a fair question to ask. However, if you keep obsessively asking the same question, it changes from being helpful to being harmful. Better for you to reflect on what you might do differently in the future than to keep using regret as an ongoing form of self-punishment.

One last point:

There are times that "Why" questions have useful answers. For example, it might be a good idea to ask your accountant, *"Why do I need to file this additional tax form?"* The answer will help you know more about the tax code. This is a world apart from the bogus "Why" question that simply hassles you (or annoys another person) without making either of you one bit smarter.

One Little Word

Why is that when you tell yourself *you want* to drive to a destination, it's fine with you? Yet, when *you have* to drive to that very same place, you feel put upon, resentful, maybe even harbor an attitude from hell.

One little word, yet what a difference! Why should this be so?

"Have to" implies coercion, as though someone is making you do something or society is telling you how you must live your life. If it feels like an affront to your individuality, what *"has"* to be done, does you in.

This applies to many areas of life.

Do you *have to* cook, or do you *want to* cook?

Do you *have to* get organized, or do you *want to* get organized?

Do you *have to* go to work, or do you *want to* go to work?

It's possible that your first response to these questions is, "I don't want to do any of those things." Yet, think again.

Though it may take time and effort to cook a meal, reflect on how good you feel when your family gathers around the dinner table. Or remind yourself about how much healthier it is than eating fast food. Or how much money you save compared to dining in fine restaurants.

Though taking the time and energy to get organized may be a hassle, admit how much better it feels to have a space that's neat and orderly rather than one that's cluttered and chaotic. Reflect on how good you feel when you can locate your glasses, keys or essential papers without first having a meltdown.

Though you might acknowledge that you really would prefer not to go to work every day, you can still admit that it's preferable to being unemployed, dependent on others or unable to afford your lifestyle. And if you

> **"And if you really do hate your job..."**

really do hate your job, wouldn't that be a sign for you to stop complaining about what you *have to do* and start looking for a job that you really *want to* do.

Even if there's something that you do only because it's a necessity (like food shopping or holiday shopping for non-shoppers), it's still better *to want* to do it (to get it over and done with) rather than continually grumble about *having to* do it.

Before I end this article *I have to* tell you (oops, *I want to* tell you) about two other words to watch out for.

Which do you think would make you feel more in charge of your own destiny? Telling yourself *"I must* make that call today" or *"I choose to* make that call today."

Which do you think would be a better motivator for you? Telling yourself "you *should* exercise" or that "you *could* exercise", then deciding what type of exercise you feel like doing.

Okay, now you know the drill. Each time you contemplate saying *I have to, I must,* or *I should,* replace these self-imposed orders with *I want to, I choose to* or *I could.* Then notice how much more empowered you feel.

Negative Self-Talk

When we talk to ourselves, many of us are harsher than our toughest critics would ever be.

Here are 4 common ways people give themselves a hard time:

Magnifying your mistakes, minimizing your accomplishments.
"I got 3 questions wrong on the test. Boy, am I stupid!"

Imagining that whatever you do will end up really bad.
"If I tried skating, I'd just make a fool out of myself."

Blaming yourself for things that are not your fault.
"My child has few friends; I don't know what I did wrong."

Name calling.
"What an idiot I am! I'm so stupid! I'm such a klutz!"

Know that you always have a choice in how you speak to yourself. Cutting out the negative self-talk is a good beginning, but not sufficient. It's also important to incorporate

> **"You always have a choice in how you speak to yourself."**

kinder, more accepting language into your inner dialogue. How often are these phrases part of your self-talk?

> *"I did a good job!"*
> *"I'm proud of myself."*
> *"It'll be tough but I can deal with it."*
> *"I made a mistake, but mistakes happen."*
> *"My hard work really paid off."*

As you can see, I'm in favor of giving yourself a break - especially if your tendency is to be too hard on yourself. If, however, for some unexplainable reason, you fear that things will go to pot if you're not your own worst critic, quit worrying. I guarantee you; there will always be someone willing to step into those shoes.

PART 3

Intimate Relationships

We fall in love; love is blind.
Sooner or later, we regain our sight, then what?

In every house of marriage, there's room for an interpreter.

Stanley Kunitz

Let us be a little humble, let us think that the truth may not perhaps lie entirely with us.

Jawaharlal Nehru

Couples in Conflict

It's not unusual for a marriage to be really two marriages -- his and hers. This is especially apparent during times of conflict.

First, let's look at the typical women's version of marital conflict, and then we'll look at the men's version.

> **"His marriage and her marriage"**

The Women's Version

"They married and lived happily ever after." Though no modern woman would admit to believing in such a fairy tale ending, nevertheless conflicts often originate and are perpetuated because the relationship is "not romantic enough" or "not the way it used to be."

Women often express disenchantment with the relationship first, saying they want to "work on the marriage" and initiate "getting help". She may feel emotionally unappreciated, distant or distressed that they do not spend enough time together or that the quality of their communication leaves much to be desired. Or, she may have specific issues with money, parenting, sex, relatives or unfinished tasks.

She questions why the relationship can't be better. Why doesn't he listen? Why doesn't he spend more time with me? Why doesn't he treat me special the way he used to?

> **Why doesn't he 'get it'?**

Some days, she may find fault with everything he does – especially if there's been a serious case of spousal deafness. Other days, she wonders if she's the one at fault. Maybe she's asking for too much. Maybe she's being too critical. Perhaps if she didn't confront him so much, he wouldn't be so defensive. Perhaps she should give him hints rather than keep hounding him. Talk to him lovingly rather than critically. Maybe then, he'll get the message. And she'll stop feeling so lonely, so angry.

She dislikes feeling like a nag, constantly reminding him to do things that he forgets. She abhors feeling like a plaintiff, accusing him of lying to her. She hates feeling like his mother, scolding him for being a bad boy. But most of all, she detests feeling like a madwoman when she's yelling, screaming, crying and feeling totally out of control.

Yet she doesn't know what else to do.

Despite some good times, their relationship has definitely deteriorated. She knows he views her as unreasonable, hysterical, and controlling. So, she backs off. But does he address any of the issues on his own? No way! Now she's not only frustrated, but depressed.

Exasperated, she turns to her friends. They listen to her. They understand. They support her. They are her allies. She no longer feels so crazy. But still, there's no resolution in sight. She's stumped. What's a woman to do?

The Men's Version

Many men are relatively content with their marriage just wishing that their wives wouldn't complain so much. Though they realize she's unhappy about certain matters, they don't get why she's *so* distraught. It seems like not much has changed since Freud asked, "What do women want?"

> **"What do women want?"**
> **Sigmund Freud**

A man's initial reaction to his wife's complaints is generally to defend himself. He does this be either denying what she accuses him of ("It's not true") or admitting it but providing a reasonable explanation, such as ("I'd like to spend more time together; it's just that work keeps me so busy.")

He may try to console his wife by telling her he's trying hard or that she shouldn't be so pessimistic or that she should focus on what he's done, not on what he hasn't done. Or he may try to explain that she worries too much or puts too much importance on insignificant details.

Yet, no matter what he does, it seems like she's still not satisfied. What does she want from him? If it's not one thing, it's another. She's still upset about things in the past that he can barely remember. Don't her resentments have an expiration date?

Keeping his emotions under control, he counters her critique rationally and if that doesn't work, he distracts himself with TV, computer, golf, work, sleep - whatever. His goal: to survive without making things worse. He knows that if he were to lose control, it would be a no-win situation. Better to remain strong, steadfast and ride out the storm.

Oh, if only this approach worked. Much to his dismay, however, she interprets his rationality and distractions as impenetrability. She feels she just can't get through to him no matter how hard she tries; he feels she just doesn't stop being dissatisfied with him.

The Way Out

What's a couple to do when their dance is so out of sync? Here are some suggestions.

> **Adopt a different attitude.** Sure when your partner pushes your button, your instinct is to defend yourself, attack or shut down. Instead, slow down. Don't react immediately. Take a deep breath. And espouse a spirit of:

- **Inquiry and Curiosity** (Ask questions and listen non-defensively as your partner explains why she feels the way she does or why he acts the way he does.)
- **Tolerance** (Cast aside your righteous indignation. Forego your pre-judgments. Agree to disagree without the certainty that your way is the only right way.)
- **Enlightenment** (Be open to learning something new, not only about your partner but also about yourself.)

React less intensely to what you don't like. He did something that bothered you. Do you get annoyed, angry or outraged? Can you accept him as he really is or are his ways intolerable to you? Your assignment, if you choose to accept it, is to moderate your response and work on letting go of your anger and animosity.

Avoid cross-complaining. When a grievance is brought to the table, do not bring up your counter complaint at that time. If you do, it will seem unfair and neither one of you will feel satisfied. First, address your partner's issue. Once you reach closure on that, then you can grumble about whatever is bothering you. Or perhaps, by that time, you won't even have a need to.

Appreciate gender differences. Men's and women's brains really are different. If you're

> **"Men's and women's brains really are different."**

telling a story and he insists you get to the bottom line quickly before you've finished your saga, know that this is not because your husband is a swine. It's simply a guy thing. And guys, your wife's need to tell you every detail of the story is not because she's a drama queen. It's simply a woman thing.

Be generous in your interpretation of your spouse's behavior. Yup, he leaves his socks on the floor, doesn't put the towel back on the rack, and leaves the toilet seat up. Is this because he wants you to be his maid? Or that he doesn't give a damn about you? Perhaps, but it's much more likely that he's simply careless, tired, or a natural born slob. If he lived by himself, he'd do the same thing. Doesn't that prove he's not doing it *to* you? Certainly, you don't have to like what he does, but if you put the worst possible interpretation on it, nothing gets resolved yet you become increasingly distressed.

Most couples in conflict focus on how they can get their partner to change. Rarely is this approach helpful. Better questions to ask are:

> *"What's this conflict really about?"*

> *"What can **I** do to change?"*

> *"How can **we** foster a better understanding of this matter?"*

> *"How can **we** work together to become more accepting of our differences?"*

> *"How can **we** develop satisfying resolutions to our couple problems?"*

If after reading this column, you still feel as stuck as ever don't hesitate to seek professional help. If you wish to save your marriage, it may be the best investment you'll ever make.

Compromises:
Graciously Or Grudgingly Given?

Gracious compromises are the lifeblood of intimate relationships; grudgingly given compromises are its death knell.

Al and Nancy were arguing over which movie to see. Finally, Nancy agreed to give in and go along with Al's choice. Though Al was pleased to be getting his way, his pleasure was short-lived. On the way to the theatre, Nancy was clearly annoyed. Try as she might, concealing her resentment was not her strong suit.

When the movie ended, her tirade began.

> *"You must be out of your mind, wanting to see such a violent movie. How selfish can you be making me sit through such bloodshed?"*

Al didn't say anything. When Nancy's anger escalated, Al typically shut down.

Nancy continued:

> *"You should have known I'd hate that kind of movie."*

Al responded:

> *"If you didn't want to go to the movie, you should've said so."*

The argument continued.

"I did say so, but you wanted to go."

"I did want to go. But if you said you wouldn't go, I would've dealt with it."

"I can't see how you can enjoy all that blood and guts. It's sick."

"It's not sick. If you don't like what I like, you think it's sick. Next time, don't agree to something and then make me pay for it."

For the next 3 hours, each retreated into resentful silence. Such is the legacy of grudgingly given compromises. Thus next time you agree to compromise, make sure that what you're agreeing to is really okay with you. If it's not, you're not doing anybody a favor.

Does that mean that you should reject compromising as an option; that everything should be done your way? In your dreams perhaps, but let's get real. What it means is that you need to learn how to compromise graciously. Here is how to make that happen:

- Listen with an open mind to what the other person wants. Don't quickly judge it as unacceptable without giving it serious thought. Even if it seems strange to you, consider the suggestion as a viable option until you have more information.

- Be open to alternatives other than your first choice. Consider second or third choices that might be okay with you.

- If you can't decide which alternative to choose, consider leaving the decision up to chance. Put several alternatives in a hat and let your partner blindly pick one.

NOW I GET IT!

- Think outside the box. If you can't find a movie both of you can agree on, reflect on how else you might spend the evening.

- Be open to serendipity -- discovering pleasurable things by accident. Sometimes you don't expect to enjoy something but it turns out to be great!

Gracious compromises may take more time and effort than grudgingly given ones, but the end result is definitely worth it!

Criticizing from Strength

"What's the matter with you? Look at your desk! How can you find anything in that mess?"

"What's so difficult about balancing a checkbook? You should keep better track of your money!"

"What's your problem with cooking dinner? Put a chicken in the oven, heat up a few veggies and dinner's ready!"

It's easy to criticize others from *our strengths*. Indeed, our ability to take care of certain tasks may be so natural that we wonder why somebody else can't *'just do it'*. The answer may seem simplistic, but the most frequent reason why others don't do what's simple for you is - *it's not so easy for them!*

Often it's hard for us to realize this because we do not give ourselves credit for being skilled at the task. It doesn't seem like a big deal. You keep your desk neat, why can't she? You balance your checkbook, why can't he? You know how to cook; we're not talking brain surgery here, what's the fuss?

If such matters were difficult for you, you would, no doubt, have more empathy for the other person. You would lament in unison as you envision the mess on your own desk. You would commiserate as you picture the state of your own checkbook. You would nod in agreement as you remember your last kitchen disaster.

Take a moment to think about one of life's tasks that you either hate doing because you're not good at it or it simply doesn't appeal to you. Now think of somebody who enjoys doing that task. If that person were critical of you for your lack of effort or enthusiasm you would probably resent it, claiming that your interests don't lie in that area or that it's impossible to keep up with everything. And you would be right; but you would now know that it doesn't quite seem like fair play when you're criticized for something that's hard for you, but easy for someone else.

If you have a *"BUT, it's different ..."* retort stuck in your throat, stifle it. Perhaps on some level, you're right. It is different. But on another level, it's simply not significant. For you still need to appreciate that what you do well is a strength, perhaps even a talent.

> **"What you do well is a strength, maybe even a talent."**

So before you judge another harshly, remember not everyone can do what you do - even when it seems to be so simple.

Two Sides to Every Story

Of course you're smart enough to know that there are two sides to every story. But is that what you're focused on when you're in the midst of a heated argument? I doubt it!

Not when the rational part of your brain has skipped town leaving the emotional part in charge. And if your emotional part is self-righteous to the core, there's no reasoning with you. You **know** what the problem is. It's clearly the other person. He's out-of-line. She's dead wrong. He has to change. She must see it my way.

Consider these examples:

> "My daughter's been hanging out with low-life friends who don't give a damn about school. I keep telling her how important it is to do well academically. She's wasting her time with these kids. But she's stubborn. No matter how many times I tell her, she doesn't get that she's ruining her life. I grounded her, but now she's threatening to run away from home. What can I do?"

> "My husband is controlling. Things have to be done his way. Half the time he doesn't even know what he's talking about, but he fakes it and acts as if he knows it all and I know nothing. I tell him how selfish he is. He doesn't even argue with me anymore. He just quietly does what he wants to do and doesn't care about what I want."

When we're on different sides of the fence, we usually try to explain to the other person what's wrong and what needs to change. If that doesn't work, we argue, threaten, withdraw, punish, nag and guess what, nothing changes.

So, what's a person to do?

Most importantly, you must listen to the other person's side of the story with the goal of | **Listen and don't "yes, but".** |

learning how he or she views the problem. Listen with an open mind. Listen non-defensively. Listen and don't "yes, but". Much to your surprise, as you listen you might hear that the other person *views you* as the cause of the problem.

Now, let's hear the other side of the two stories.

"My mom is always on my case. She judges my friends without even knowing them. If she doesn't like the way they look or they're not honor students, she doesn't even give them a chance. She's such a hypocrite! She thinks if she grounds me, I'll abandon my friends. I can't let her control my life. I'd rather run away from home than let her bully me."

"My wife is forever telling me the way things should be. She reads an article, talks with her friends, watches Oprah and that makes her an expert. She looks at me as the dummy who knows nothing. So I just keep quiet and do as I please. I know that drives her crazy but if I argue my point, she counter argues wearing me down with her incessant explaining. She thinks I'm controlling but she's the one who can't tolerate anybody doing anything different from the 'right' way - which just happens to be 'her' way."

Quite different stories!

To move beyond gridlock, you must be ready to listen *respectfully* to another's story.

As you do so, you may find yourself conceding a point or two instead of simply repeating your story and hardening your position. Recognizing the merit in another's viewpoint makes it more likely that you can arrive at a good resolution to what once seemed like an intractable problem.

Is Your Relationship in Trouble?

"She's never ready on time."
"He's always on the computer."
"She never puts the cap back on the toothpaste."
"He leaves his socks and underwear on the floor."

These are the complaints of a *happily married* couple. Other couples, in contrast, may look like they really have it together until the day they shock even their best friends with the announcement that they're getting divorced.

Clearly, the health of a relationship is not always evident to outsiders. Moreover, it may not even be evident to the people in the relationship.

Sometimes, you just don't know if your own relationship is in jeopardy or if it has simply hit a few bumps in the road. Of course, time will tell - nothing stays the same; things either get better or worse.

> **"Time will tell; nothing stays the same."**

But wouldn't it be helpful if you could assess relationship symptoms much like people do with medical symptoms? That way you can either reassure yourself that your differences are no big deal. Or learn that they are precursors of serious trouble and that it would be prudent for you to address them tout de suite.

Here are 4 telltale signs that indicate critical trouble ahead:

111

Interpreting your spouse's behavior as a terrible character flaw.
It's not just what your spouse does (or doesn't do) that creates problems; it's also how *you* interpret the behavior. The more damning your interpretation is to your partner's character, the more your relationship is in jeopardy.

If you interpret leaving dishes in the sink as evidence that she never does anything right or that she doesn't give a damn about anyone else except herself, your relationship is in big time trouble. If your interpretation is that she's frequently forgetful or careless, you can breathe easy; no major problem here.

Frequent cross-complaining.
Cross-complaining is when one person makes a complaint and the other person makes a quick counter compliant rather than addressing what the first person has brought up. For instance, he comes home from work, saying "What a tough day I had." Before he can say anything else, she responds, "Ha, you think your day was tough; my day was worse than yours." The upshot: Feeling discounted ("my problem doesn't count") and alienated ("what I experienced doesn't matter").

Another form of cross-complaining is an abrupt shift into what's wrong with you as a counter to a complaint about what's wrong with me. "You forgot to put napkins on the table" turns into, "Yeah; well you forgot to call your sister." This is especially damaging to the relationship when the counter complaint gets nasty, vindictive or expansive, as in: "And you never do anything I ask you to do; you've got some nerve complaining about me when you're the biggest screw-up there is."

Treating your spouse with contempt or disdain.
Obviously, you cannot hope for a healthy relationship
if you're treating your spouse with disdain.
Sometimes such an attitude is obvious; other times,
it's more subtle. Be aware of contempt that takes the
form of:

    -Disgust with what he did.
    -Scorning her take on the matter.
    -Patronizing him.
    -Lecturing her.
    -Rolling your eyes.

    -Ridiculing what he said.
    -Rejecting an apology.
    -Being intolerant of mistakes.
    -Creating nonnegotiable demands.
    -Threatening divorce.

**Not enough good times to counterbalance the bad
ones.**
It's a sad fact, but true, that negative experiences tend
to linger longer in memory than positive ones. Hence,
for a relationship to thrive, a couple needs to make
sure there are many more good experiences to
balance out just one bad one. And if the bad one is a
whopper, only time and sincere effort to rebuild trust
will help heal the relationship.

"You've Got a Point"

It's not unusual for arguments to bring out the worst in each individual. As you become entrenched in your position, you may look at your partner as someone who will never 'get it'. Beware of thinking that you have a monopoly on the truth, while the other person is capricious, stupid or just plain wrong.

Such arguments are models of zero sum games. There's a winner and a loser. While this is a fine model for competitive sports, it's a miserable model for personal relationships. To change a zero sum game into a positive sum game (win-win), you need to stop repeating your own position and start believing that *something* about the other person's position is valid.

The simple phrase *"you've got a point"* will help you accomplish this.

Telling the other person that he's got a point does not mean that you're caving in or giving up. Rather, it's creating a climate for respectful communication - despite high-powered emotions or wide differences in perspective. Respectful communication makes it easier to negotiate workable compromises.

Listen to the difference between these two short scenarios:

"We should buy new furniture for the living room. The old furniture is looking shabby."

"No way. We can't afford it and there's nothing wrong with what we have."

"I expected you to say that. You're so tight with money; you never want to spend anything."

"Hey, big spender, if you were making the money, maybe then we'd have more money to spend."

Now notice what happens when there's just a little validation of the other person's viewpoint injected into the dialogue.

"We should buy new furniture for the living room. The old furniture is looking shabby."

"You've got a point *but I don't think we can afford it now and the furniture doesn't really look that bad."*

"I expected you to say that. You never want to spend anything. But you've got a point, I know money is tight."

"If you really want new furniture, waiting till next year will make it easier on our budget."

"I could look now but not buy till later. You know how long it takes me to make up my mind anyway."

I often think that what we really crave from others is nothing more than validation:
- yes, what you think makes sense
- yes, what you feel is genuine
- yes, what you want is understandable

When we receive such validation, we find ourselves becoming less rigid, no longer needing to drive our point home relentlessly and harshly.

As you begin to make *"you've got a point"* a part of your conversation, you will discover that you can:

- Consider the merits of another's position without immediately being antagonistic to it.

- Recognize that you don't need to polarize differences, making one of you right, the other wrong.

- Be more considerate toward your partner's feelings as you make your point.

- Be more open to finding creative solutions to your differences.

An added attractive bonus:

As you validate your partner's position, you will likely discover that your partner is more open to validating yours.

Learning From Those Who Distress You

What if I told you that you could learn a thing or two from those very people who distress you the most? And that the characteristics which you can't stand about someone might be just what you should respect, maybe even emulate.

> **"Everything that irritates us about others can lead us to an understanding of ourselves."**
> **Carl Jung**

Now I know it's terribly hard to give credence to an alternative way of thinking when you're certain that you're right and the other person's wrong. And yet, if you're sharing your life with this other person, what choice do you have? You've probably tried shutting out her ideas or instructing him in the error of his ways. And where has that gotten you?

So, as a creative experiment, consider seeing if you can learn something from this person who is the source of so much of your distress. Here's an example:

> Eleanor can't stand when her husband Ed is inflexible with the kids. He won't take any backtalk from them and doesn't hesitate to mete out punishments that the kids complain are too harsh. Eleanor firmly believes that he should have more patience and be more lenient with them. She is so upset with him over this matter that it has led to serious marital discord.

117

Despite Eleanor's take on the matter, what if she entertained the belief that maybe *some* aspect of Ed's style of disciplining might be worthy of consideration? She admits that she's often exhausted trying to satisfy her kids' never ending needs. And she's annoyed with their incessant whining when they don't get what they want. Maybe, it would be good for her to learn to set limits with them and become a stricter parent herself.

Similarly, if Ed could entertain the belief that he might learn something from his wife (whom he believes is too easy-going with the kids), good things might happen for him too. Perhaps he wouldn't have to always feel like the heavy. And it would feel good to be closer to his kids instead of always finding fault with them. Even if he didn't want to give up his no-nonsense style of disciplining, couldn't he still emulate his wife's nurturing communication style?

Those who distress us actually have much to teach us. To find out what that might be for you, search for *what's right* about the other person's approach (even if it's just a little thing) rather than just tallying off all the ways it's wrong.

Are You Ready For Marriage?

Not everybody is ready for marriage - no matter how much you are in love or how mature you are in other areas of life. To create and maintain a healthy marriage, you must possess these basic relationship skills:

You need to be able to separate emotionally from your family of origin.
Though, hopefully, you will maintain a close and loving relationship with your family, you won't be calling on your folks to back you up or to referee an argument with your spouse. Nor will you have the mindset that the way your parents approached a task was by definition the "right" way and anything different is the wrong way.

If you are divorced or widowed, you will also need to separate emotionally from your first marriage. Strong residual feelings of love, anger, guilt or resentment can interfere with the blossoming of a new relationship.

You must be able to create a "we" feeling in your relationship.
Once married, you are a couple - not just two separate individuals. I'm not suggesting that there's no room for individuality in your relationship nor do you both need to view things the same way. But you do need to have a sense of how you as a couple handle the business of life. Ask yourself, "What is *our* way of tackling household chores? *Our* way to pay the bills? *Our* way to spend leisure time? *Our* way to be

intimate? *Our* way to raise the kids?"

An example: If a couple has different styles of managing their money, they may decide to have separate bank accounts. He may balance his checkbook to the penny; she may never balance hers. But as long as they have agreed as a couple that this works for them, it becomes *their* way of handling the money. If they cannot agree that this is okay, and are always battling which way is right, there is no "we" agreement here.

You must be able to cope with conflict.
Even the best of relationships are not conflict free. Hence, you need to have a basic knowledge of how to handle conflict. How good are you at listening to your partner's point of view without ridicule or disrespect? How skilled are you at presenting your point-of-view without righteous indignation or rage? How open are you to compromising graciously instead of grudgingly?

If you know that you have lots to learn about coping with conflict, that's okay. However, if you believe that any and all conflict is your partner's fault and has nothing to do with your responses, then you're simply not ready for marriage.

You must be able to cope with the inevitable crises of life without turning on each other.
Hopefully, there will be lots of wonderful times in store for you. But there will also be tough

> **"Every crisis has the potential to hurt or heal a marriage."**

times that can strain any marriage. Some of these may be expected, such as becoming a parent. Others, however, such as major illness or serious financial difficulties may come as a complete surprise. Every crisis has the potential to hurt or heal a marriage, depending on whether you face the crisis together or turn on each other with blame and shame.

A successful marriage requires the maturity to postpone gratification, compromise graciously, and cope creatively with difficulties.

Are you ready?

Hopeless Romantics

Romance is addicting. It makes one feel so loved, so special. What could be bad about another soul being infatuated with you, simply because of your good looks, stimulating ideas, or infectious smile?

Though at the onset romance may seem seductively sweet, there can be a downside to it – especially when the hopeless romantic has a disposition that can become hazardous to your health. Here are traits to be wary of:

Impulsivity:
She wants you now! She can't wait! You're the dream guy she's been looking for. Though the impulsive part of you may long to say "yes, yes, yes" to this relationship believing you have at long last met your soul mate, you'd be wise to listen to the smart part of your brain. This part should be flashing warning signals that something's not right here. How can she be so in love with you when she doesn't even know you? How can you commit to her when you barely know her either?

A Need for Control:
All the attention you receive may feel very flattering in the beginning.

> **"her need to control you…"**

Flowers sent to your office! E-mail love notes! Surprise visits! Every day is Valentine's Day. But just wait until you experience the flip side of the coin - her need to control you, her jealous nature, her over-the-top expectations. The attention has now become pressure - pressure for making her your #1 priority at the expense of friends, family, interests and even work.

Sudden Mood Swings:
It starts off great. She's loving and considerate in a way no other woman has ever been. Your heart melts. Your spirit soars. All is right with the world. Then one day she does an about-face from sweet and loving to brooding and angry. This happens in a matter of minutes. You wonder what's wrong. Somehow, she makes you feel responsible for her mood change. Perhaps you didn't pay enough attention to her, didn't satisfy her, didn't do what was expected of you. You have fallen off the pedestal she put you on and now you get to pay the price.

Though a few hot and heavy romances blossom into stable and loving relationships, most are short-lived - remaining a pleasant memory. Some, however, become abusive when the neurotic need for attachment and intensity cannot abide by the realities of everyday living.

A caveat:
The impulsive, controlling, jealous, blaming, mood swinging romantic can be either male or female.

Love Scripts

Is it just a lucky break that your friend seems to have a great marriage while you have one troubled relationship after another?

Is it just an amazing coincidence that the same difficulties you had with your parent(s) you now have with your spouse?

Did you swear you would never get involved with another alcoholic because of his self-destructive tendencies, and then find yourself involved with another addictive personality, like a workaholic or a spendaholic?

> **"Is our destiny doomed?"**

What's going on here? Do we have free will in our relationships or is our destiny doomed, much like a Greek tragedy?

The answer: A bit of both.

Most Americans pride themselves on their independence, believing that they can "reinvent" themselves whenever they wish. This belief may be more hype than truth for though people can change, it's particularly difficult to do so when under the influence of a *love script.*

A love script, much like a theatrical script, is essentially a blueprint for the dramatic enactment of a love story. First, there's the beginning, then the struggle and finally the outcome.

Here are two examples of love scripts:

Rescuer Script:

The Beginning: She meets a guy who is going through a tough time. She feels drawn to him. It makes her feel good to be there for him and help him resolve his problems.

The Struggle: Though she'd like to help him, it's turning out to be more difficult than she thought. He has one problem after another. She feels frustrated, confused. Is she helping him too much? Is he using her? Is she an enabler? Though she wants to be there for him, she didn't believe she was signing up for full-time, long-term rescue duty.

The Outcome: Either she will keep hanging in there, continuing to rescue him each time he messes up. Or she will change her script by refusing to play the rescue role, seeing if he can extricate himself from his own difficulties. Or, she will end the relationship. However, unless she becomes cognizant of her love script and modifies it, it won't be long till she finds herself a new person to rescue.

Fairy Tale Script:

The Beginning: He meets someone who is his dream girl. She's beautiful, caring, gentle, kind. She will be his perfect partner.

The Struggle: He's now discovering qualities about her that he didn't know before. He tries to downplay the times she gets up in arms over relatively small matters. He tries to calm her down when she's upset about what he did or didn't do. He's disappointed; he longs for that delightful feeling he had when he first fell in love. Is he expecting too much from her? Is she not the dream girl he believed her to be?

The Outcome: Fairy tale scripts nosedive once real life issues intrude. Either he will continue to feel disappointed with his dream girl. Or he will find a way to transform his fantasy script into a reality script. Or he will end the relationship and search again for a new dream girl.

If your relationships keep having the same problems no matter who your partner is, you're undoubtedly hooked into a script that satisfies some important emotional need. Give your script a name. See what the need is. Be aware of what problems the script causes and what the typical outcome is. Then see if you can generate a new script that is less rigid, less starry-eyed and more multi-dimensional.

Myth or Reality?

Some ideas we accept as true simply because everybody else seems to believe they're true. When examined more closely, however, we recognize that they're more myth than reality. With that in mind, I'd like you to forget everything you've ever learned about how to make an intimate relationship work and approach this column with an open mind.

Here are three ideas about intimate relationships that are generally taken as fact:

-If an intimate relationship is to succeed, you must have two people who are constantly willing to work at it.

-Increased communication is the key to improving relationships.

-If you care deeply about your relationship, you will prove it by making whatever changes are necessary.

Though these ideas have a kernel of truth to them, they are far from the whole truth. Here is a more realistic version of the three "facts" just mentioned.

Two people who are always working on their relationship will become exhausted from all this work.
Sure, giving importance to your relationship is necessary but once it's perceived as "work", resentment prevails. Think of other areas in your

life that require constant work. Doesn't it become burdensome? Don't you wish you could escape it all? Intimate relationships should be enjoyable, relating to each other should be fun, being with each other should be stimulating, not exhausting.

Increased communication often makes things worse.

Unless you learn *better* communication skills, more communication may just mean more arguing, more hostility. Do you really need to hear once again how you did

> **"More communication may just mean more arguing, more hostility."**

something wrong, how you didn't listen, or how you're insensitive? It is **the quality** (not the quantity) of communication that invariably needs to be improved. And since patterns of communication are so entrenched, most couples need professional assistance to become aware of how their communication skills are off the mark and what can be done to improve them.

A person can care deeply about a relationship, yet have difficulty making the changes that his partner would like.

Do not question the sincerity of a partner's caring, just because he is having difficulty altering his behavior or changing her ingrained mind-sets. If you are expecting an extreme and immediate makeover from your partner, you are being unfair as well as setting yourself up for disappointment. Try instead to notice the smaller changes that your partner may be making to please you, rather than harping on the larger, more unattainable changes.

A Cliffs Notes understanding of a relationship is simple and unadorned. If you are looking for a more profound understanding of a relationship, you must take the time to immerse yourself in the subtleties of what is happening, both on and below the surface.

Emotional Infidelity and the Internet

Do you get an adrenaline rush when you're chatting online with that special someone? Do you share more of your dreams, fears and fantasies with your cyber pal than with your spouse? Do you keep your correspondence with your "friend" a secret? If so, you may be having an emotional affair, despite the lack of sexual contact.

What exactly is an emotional affair? Does it only happen over the Internet? Why should it count as an affair if it's "only" emotional? Can't people of the opposite sex be friends?

> **"What exactly is an emotional affair?"**

Though emotional affairs have always existed, they're much more likely to happen now, given the ease of maintaining a secret relationship over the Internet. Many connections begin innocently enough but change in nature over time as the correspondence becomes more intimate.

Though married people often have friends of both genders, a different dynamic emerges when the friendship is really an emotional affair. Energy, attention, support and intimacy within the couple relationship tend to wane as these factors become a more significant part of the relationship with the Internet partner.

Pretty soon it's easy to feel that only this friend "understands you", "is special" or "gives you the attention you deserve." In comparison, your spouse may seem like an unappreciative bore or a taskmaster who is chronically complaining about one thing or another.

Excluding your spouse from all or certain aspects of the relationship creates a pattern of deceit. Indeed, if a spouse discovers what's really going on, the typical response is identical to that of finding out about a sexual affair: hurt, anger, betrayal and a loss of trust, respect, safety and feeling special.

If you're involved in an emotional affair, here is some advice for you:

Stop lying to yourself.
Don't keep saying this is "just a friend" if it has gone beyond friendship. If you're struggling with where to draw the line, err on the side of caution, not on the side of recklessness.

If you have a perpetual need for being admired or adored, you may be acting out a neurotic need for pure and unconditional love.
Rather than jeopardizing your real life relationship, take time to explore the insecurities and vulnerabilities that are fueling these needs.

An emotional affair is often a signal that there are matters that need to be addressed within your marriage.
Sometimes, it's simply lethargy or laziness that has stripped the enthusiasm and excitement from a relationship. Other times there are more fundamental issues that need to be confronted. Regardless of which it is, if you care about keeping your marriage intact, don't let an Internet relationship destroy it.

In the long run, the rewards you reap will be more gratifying if your best friend is the friend you wake up with every morning.

PART 4

The Art of Parenting

Parenting is more art than science. But like art,
we need to acquire the skills
that give rise to great performance.

*Children begin by loving their parents; as they grow older
they judge them; sometimes they forgive them.*

Oscar Wilde

*Before I got married I had six theories about bringing up
children; now I have six children, and no theories.*

John Wilmot

Entitled Kids, Defensive Parents

We have been in a new era of child rearing for quite sometime now. This new era was supposed to be an improvement over the old one, in which disciplining children was based on an unreflective use of fear, punishment and "do it, because I said so."

Today's parents seek to raise their kids in a more enlightened way. They want their children to feel empowered, self-confident and self-assured. Many parents, however, are getting more than they bargained for and are shocked when their entitled kids act in an insolent, arrogant manner. Overwhelmed with self-doubt, parents find themselves on the defensive, not sure how to respond to this monster they created.

> **"Many parents are getting more than they bargained for..."**

Here's a typical example:

> The parents were at their wits' end trying to understand what happened to Heather, their 12-year-old daughter. Her overwhelmed mom said, *"She used to be sweet and caring. She loved showing me her school work and telling me about her day. Now, she's completely changed and is totally out of control!"*

Mom then described the latest incident.

> *"Heather, get your books off the couch and put them in your room."*

> *"Why? I don't need to."*

NOW I GET IT!

"Yes, you do need to. I'm asking you to do it."

"No, it's stupid. I don't want to do it."

"Heather, you're not the only one who lives here. This house is a mess and I want it cleaned up."

"So clean it up."

"Stop being fresh. You're asking for it."

"Get off my case. Every time you see me watching TV, you get a bug up your ass. What's your problem, mom? Why don't you get a life?"

In most households of yesteryear, this conversation would have been unthinkable. If perchance it occurred, the child would have received a severe punishment or beating. Yet, the most amazing thing about this type of dialogue is that it's not that unusual in today's families.

The notion of entitlement has dramatically changed the parent-child relationship, leading kids to believe that:

- They are their parents equal.
- They should be entitled to make their own decisions.
- They should get what they want.
- They should show respect only if (they think) you deserve it.
- They have a right to talk back to adults in any manner they choose.
- They should be able to argue incessantly until their parents relent.

Many parents are desperate to gain back the control. After "trying everything", they end up concluding that nothing works. It's hard to maintain the upper hand when:

- punishing your child begets an arrogant retort,

- lecturing your child begets a 'who cares' shrug,

- explaining what you want begets a contemptuous comeback,

- enforcing a rule begets soap opera theatrics.

Frustrated, parents may end up behaving in a way that makes them feel ashamed of themselves - cursing at their kids, yelling obscenities, slapping them, saying awful things that they later regret. Or, parents may stifle their anger to prevent such a scene - feeling ashamed of what they're feeling, embarrassed that they're the parents of such an out-of-control kid.

Then, just as they are ready to disown their offspring, their kid makes a turnaround – speaking respectfully, acting nicely, even showing concern about their family. That's when parents become increasingly confused. Have they exaggerated the situation? Is this just a stage that their child is going through? Will their relationship with their kid ever improve?

For parents who deal on a daily basis with the needs of entitled kids, life can feel like a never ending struggle. Hence the need for ground rules to maintain a modicum of control. Here are the basics:

Don't allow your child to bully you, call you nasty names or otherwise treat you disrespectfully.
If he does, you must divert the conversation, making the manner in which he speaks to you the new topic of conversation. If he invokes freedom of speech issues, ("I can say what I want; it's a free country"), don't take the bait. Tell him in a strong voice that you won't tolerate being spoken to in that way.

Having stated your position, you don't need to go into a full blown lecture. He knows what you mean. A child, however, models what he hears. Thus, you will have no leg to stand on if you curse him but expect him to abide by different rules. Today's kids don't buy the argument that it's okay for you because you're the adult but not okay for them because they're the kids.

If your child backs off or (miracle of miracles) apologizes, congratulations! You've made your point. But if he keeps speaking to you disrespectfully, walk away. If he follows you, do not interact. Your message, "When you speak to me respectfully, I'll be ready to listen," needs to be reinforced.

Your responsibility as a parent is to make reasonable and age-appropriate rules.
Parents set the rules, kids resist the rules. Though you may entertain a discussion about modifying the rules, do not simply cave in to their demands. If you do, the power structure of the family becomes inverted. The result: Turmoil and Trouble, with a capital T.

Don't punish your child when you're feeling out-of-control.
If you do, you're sure to regret what you've done. When you feel calmer, you'll recognize that you have gotten yourself into a quandary. Let the punishment slide and you weaken your authority. Keep the punishment intact when you both know it's foolish and you lose your credibility. Best to create a punishment after you've given it thought. If possible, make it educational and enforceable. For instance: Which do you think would be a better punishment for breaking curfew? No TV for 2

weeks or composing a 2 page essay on the responsibilities of a parent plus a mandatory discussion on the topic.

Don't allow yourself to be manipulated by your child's half-truths.
You can listen to your child, hear him out, and even respect his take on a matter. But don't give in just because your child is grinding you down. Entitled kids are all budding lawyers who know how to present their case, stand on their rights and denigrate you and your position. Don't be intimidated. Think before you respond. If you need more time to come up with a response, say that. If the diatribe is getting out of hand, end the communication with a simple but direct, "That's it; conversation's over."

Fake confidence, even if you don't feel it.
Should you require your child to put away her laundry or let her just leave it on the floor? Should you give your child permission to stay home from school if he claims he's got a headache or make him go anyway? It's your call. No need to come across as an ogre, with no room for negotiation or input. But you do need to be in the parental role and make a judgment. Don't be indecisive or wishy-washy. If you are, your child will use your weakness against you.

Because you are the parent, doesn't mean you need to make all the decisions.
Indeed, if you want to encourage responsibility in your child, you need to let him make some of his own decisions. At times, it's appropriate to tell your child that you have confidence in his judgment, saying, "It's up to you to figure it out," or "It's your call." Transferring the decision to your age

appropriate child is very different from allowing him to usurp the authority from you.

Let your child experience the natural consequences of her actions.
Do not protect your child from the consequences of her behavior. Your daughter doesn't put her dirty clothes in the hamper, she doesn't have clean clothes. Your son failed his English class, he goes to summer school. Yes, you may need to suffer through a tantrum in which they complain about how unfair it is, but stick to your guns. Short-term appeasement invariably creates long-term regrets.

Indirect communication may be more effective than direct communication that's ignored.
Instead of repeatedly saying "You've got to study more," or "Clean up your room," try a more indirect statement like, "Studying more can help you boost your grades," or "It's easier to find things when you organize your stuff." Then say nothing. Don't spell it out for him. Let less be more. A short circuitous message can be more meaningful than hours of yelling, nagging, and lecturing.

Compliment your child without going overboard.
Simple sentences, like "I admire the way you handled that," or "Good grade, way to go," are best. If your entitled child already thinks she's the greatest, you don't want to gush approval and reinforce her thinking about how wonderful she is. Yet, you also don't want to refrain from complimenting her, even though your relationship is strained.

Finally, make sure your child views you as a well-rounded person, not just as a parent whose primary job is to satisfy your kid's every whim. If your family is overly child-centered, you are feeding into the dynamic of the entitled child. Enlarge your interests. Instead of talking only about your child's day, tell your child something about your day. And make it interesting! If all you talk about are the chores you've done, you'll sound like a drone. Instead, talk about an interest you're nurturing, a friend you met, a trip you're planning.

If your mind is drawing a blank, it's way past due for you to put time and energy into growing yourself.

A Guide to Surviving the Teen Years

Are you a parent of an adolescent? Are you so upset with your teen that you want to enroll him in the *"Witless Protection Program"*? Do you hope that a new identity would result in his renouncing

"The Witless Protection Program"

his risky behavior? Or that it just might get her to shut her mouth and show some respect?

You're not alone. I've heard, however, that there's a twenty year waiting list for this program. So, unless you're well connected, you've simply got to do what you've got to do to survive those teen years.

Here are some thoughts on the subject.

First, the good news: Know that some behaviors that may seem disrespectful when viewed through a parental lens may actually be an expression of healthy adolescent development.

Here's a story to illustrate this point.

> When my oldest son Brian was 15 years old, he overheard his 10-year-old brother asking me for permission to have a friend sleep over. Something about Danny's request must have rubbed Brian the wrong way, for a short time afterwards I overheard him admonishing his brother for being so spineless with his request. "Next time", Brian said, "tell Mom – 'Mitch is sleeping over tonight, OK?' and say it, if you can, when you're halfway out the door."

How should you as a parent assess Brian's communication? Is it disrespectful – teaching a younger brother how to dodge authority? Or is it nurturing – teaching a younger brother how to be more assertive and 'become a man'? My answer: the latter, hands down.

Next time your teen acts in a manner that you think is out-of-line, consider if there's another way to think about it. Might he actually be asserting himself in a way that would be respected if he were an adult? Might this acting out be a necessary precursor to his becoming a self-assured grown-up who knows his way around a system?

Admittedly, many adolescents assert themselves in an over-the-top manner, so their parents experience them as more aggressive than assertive. In these situations, it's better to suggest ways that your teen might sandpaper his rough edges rather than simply raking him over the coals for being disrespectful.

Now for the bad news: Many teens lack good judgment, having little regard for real life perils. Thinking they know it all, they dismiss the possible consequences of risky behavior. Now, of course, teens have always acted without caution and been rebellious. But for the most part they did it behind their parents' back, having the decency to concoct a story they swore was true.

> "I was just holding the drugs for my friend."

> "We haven't done any more than kissed."
> "Of course, my friend's parents will be home."

And parents, even if they felt uneasy, could choose to believe what they wanted to believe about their kids.

Today's rebellious teens, however, are more likely to be in your face:

> "Of course, I'm smoking pot. There's nothing wrong with

it. You're such a hypocrite. You smoked pot when you were a kid; now you don't want me to do it. I hate you!"

"You've no right to check on where I go on the Internet. I'll do what I want to do."

"Oral sex is no big deal; it's not even sex. What's your hang-up?"

These kids blur the distinction between what they're exposed to (on Websites, Blogs, music and TV) and how one lives life. Propped up by their sub-culture, they reject not only their parents' values but also the values they believed in just a few years ago.

So, how does a parent survive these teen years? Here are some suggestions:

Know that there is a natural tension between adolescents who crave adventure and parents whose paramount interest is in keeping their kids safe.
Your goal should be to encourage an adventurous spirit, yet make sure that your teen is aware of realistic dangers that may result from risky behavior. Do not, however, expect your kid to live a 'safe' life in order to quell your own anxiety. Instead, teach them to think critically.

Know that you have a right (even an obligation) to create rules and to express your disapproval with out-of-line behavior.
But it's best to create the rules without hysteria or empty threats. Reflect on what leverage you do have and use it, especially to gain power when your rules are trampled upon.

Despite your teen's over-the-top behavior, it's a

good sign if she's initiating conversation.
Take her communication to mean that she wants to maintain a relationship with you. Respond to her in an affirmative way, such as: "I'm glad we're talking, even though what you're telling me is upsetting and uncomfortable for me. It's easier for me to hear you, when you drop the attitude."

When things are relatively calm, try to engage your teen in a dialogue.
Don't just keep telling your teen what she should or shouldn't be doing. If you believe she's tried pot, ask her specific questions, such as: "What's it like for you when you get high? Did you ever have a bad reaction? What would you do if you did? How would you handle it if you're pressured to do something you don't want to do?" Such questions can be asked either all at once (if your teen is into it) or at different times (if she's viewing you as the grand inquisitor).

If your teen does respond to your questions, listen without lecturing.
To get to know what's going on in your kid's life, you need to be able to shed your own skin and inhabit your teen's for a while. If your kid tells you what's really going on, your initial impulse may be to ground him for the rest of his natural life. But remember that the bottom line here is to keep the communication open so that you can guide your teen toward making good choices while inculcating him with good values.

Whatever Works

We can be so full of ourselves, assuming that we know what should be done in a specific situation. Once we're in the situation, however, we begin to recognize that things are so much more complex than we imagined them to be.

Take for example, being a parent. Before you had kids, chances are you had some definitive ideas about how you would raise your kids.

Lucky you; you were blessed with ignorance.

Now, that you're older and wiser, however, you probably know the following:

- You now know that despite your best intentions, family life often comes down to creating ad hoc compromises so that tasks get accomplished and the little people as well as the big people get most of their needs met.

- You now know that you live in a world in which you don't make the rules by which you must abide. If you did, you wouldn't even think about giving your kids homework on the weekends nor would you schedule one child's activity to directly conflict with another's.

- You now know that though family life from afar may seem picture perfect, close up it feels much like chaos – not only external chaos (the stuff, the toys, the clothes) but also internal chaos (the worries, the pressures, the schedules). And despite trying really, really hard, something always manages to slip through the cracks.

- You now recognize that the desire to create order is a constant struggle. You thought that housekeeping was difficult before kids – ha! Now, despite lowering your expectations, a working system of order and organization seems to always be just out of reach.

- You now know that your wish to impose order is not only about housekeeping. It's also about holding on to your identity. It's a struggle to organize your day so that it does not slip away without doing something meaningful for your personal and professional growth.

As a mature person with sophistication and depth, you now know how infinitely complex family life is. Though you try to live up to your principles about how things 'should' be, you also acknowledge that the best solution to real life predicaments is often - *whatever works.*

> **"...the best solution to real life predicaments is often – whatever works."**

When you hear others speak critically about this approach, you smile serenely. For you now know that to be absolutely certain about how things should be, you must know very little about the way things are.

Mistakes and "Pockets of Ignorance"

There is one valuable gift that all parents, rich or poor, can give their children. It costs nothing, yet kids yearn for it. Ironically, that gift is also the one thing many parents refuse to give their kids because they believe it's inappropriate or wrong for them to do so.

This precious gift consists of two parts:

The right to make mistakes - without feeling embarrassed or afraid. Being able to make a mistake without being ridiculed or putdown is essential for one's self-confidence to blossom. Indeed, if a child is not making mistakes, it's likely he's avoiding taking chances that would be good for his continuing development. Big difference between raising your child to be cautious and raising your child to be fearful.

The right to not know - without being made to feel stupid. 'Pockets of ignorance' is what I call that bit of information, understanding or skill that one lacks that has nothing to do with basic smarts. Such ignorance is best explained by a lack of interest, lack of experience, or a bit of confusion. Kids that are not granted the 'right to not know' work hard to cover up their ignorance, always on guard to make sure that what they don't know doesn't surface.

Mark was raised in **a blame-oriented family.** Do something wrong and there was all hell to pay. Mark remembers being blamed and shamed for the smallest infractions. "What's wrong with you? You're a moron! You can't do anything right? Nine years old and you still can't pour a glass of milk without making a mess." Mark admitted that those zingers still resonate with him though they took place more than 20 years ago. He confessed, "Even today, despite my being a successful businessman, when I make a mistake I feel like a complete idiot. No doubt about it, that intimidated kid still lives inside me."

Even Jason, who was raised in an **overly child-centered family**, learned that mistakes were unacceptable. "Of course, I didn't tell my parents what was going on in my life," said Jason. "Why should I? My dad, the know-it-all, would lecture me about how I should have done things differently. After the lecture, the inquisition would roll in. How did it happen? What was I thinking? What did I learn from this experience? How could I have done things differently? And my mom was even worse. She's the worried type, becoming hysterical that I could have been killed, kidnapped, or injured."

Kids who feel okay about not knowing can freely ask questions, admit their ignorance and learn in the process. Kids who feel humiliated about not knowing try to conceal their ignorance, feeling bad about themselves if any lack of knowledge is discovered.

Parents, next time you're looking for a gift to give your kids, let it be the gift of acceptance. Mistakes and 'pockets of ignorance' are nothing to be ashamed of.

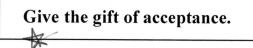

Give the gift of acceptance.

And while you're at it, why not consider giving this gift to yourself as well. After all, inside each of us is a little kid who may be just as vulnerable today as she was in years past.

NOW I GET IT!

Same Parents, Different Parenting

Is what you remember what really occurred?

According to Gary, his father was a cold and distant man with a bad temper. "He would get angry easily and never let me explain anything. It was his way or the highway."

Gary's younger sister Denise had a softer perspective. "I thought my father had a rough exterior but a kind heart. Sure, sometimes he'd get angry and yell but when he saw that I was hurting, he'd calm down and talk gently to me."

When Gary heard Denise's words, he couldn't believe it. "Are you kidding? Our father was a stubborn man with a mean streak. Forget about listening to me or caring about what I thought. He never even gave me a chance to explain myself. He'd accuse and convict me in two seconds flat."

Denise believes her brother is being unfair to their father - exaggerating the negative, minimizing the positive. Gary believes Denise is living in la-la land, distorting the reality of their childhood.

Why should there be such divergent perspectives from two siblings who were brought up in the same household? There are the obvious reasons. A son might be treated differently from a daughter; an older child differently from a younger one. But there's another more subtle reason that's an important factor.

Children's own personalities have a strong, often unrecognized impact on how their parents treat them.

Gary admits that he has a confrontational personality. "I took pride in not letting my father get to me. When he lost his cool, I became just as bullheaded as he was. At that point, I didn't care what he did to me."

Denise, on the other hand, described her personality this way. "I wanted my father's approval. When he was upset with me, I was upset with myself. I felt guilty when I disappointed him. I've always been the sensitive type and would try hard to please him."

Most of us believe that parents should treat their kids equally. But what if the kids don't act the same way? Let's face it. If you had a sweet, compliant personality that sought out your parent's approval, it's likely you would have received more positive stroking than an independent or defiant sibling. And if you were the stubborn type - refusing to give in no matter what - no doubt you would have elicited more power struggles than a more yielding sibling.

> "But what if the kids don't act the same way?"

Hence, instead of fanning the flames of a Freudian fire by faulting your parents for whatever went wrong in your life, chill out. Look at the broader picture, taking note of how your personality style might have contributed to the conflicts within the relationship.

Bring Back the Guilt

If your parents marinated you with guilt your whole childhood, you may have vowed to never repeat the pattern with your kids. As Nina says, *"Guilt is manipulative. It made me neurotic. I won't do that to my kids. It's not fair to burden them with guilt."*

If you took that vow seriously, it's a good chance that your kids are acting out, demanding, rude, and walking all over you. If this is what's happening, you might want to consider bringing back the guilt.

> **"...consider bringing back the guilt."**

Not an overabundance of guilt.
"I know you're doing something wrong; you always do."

Not heavy-handed guilt.
"If you weren't so bad, I wouldn't have to punish you all the time."

Not unfair guilt.
"Look what you made me do. I wouldn't have dropped the plate if you didn't get me so nervous."

--- But Healthy Guilt.
"I told you to stop playing ball in the house. You didn't listen. Now you've broken the lamp and I'm upset with your bad behavior."

As children mature, a well-developed sense of guilt is important for their well-being. This is true because parents have less and less direct control over their children in these ways.

Physically: Though it's no picnic to pick up a screaming 3-year-old and walk out of the store because he's behaving badly, it's quite impossible to do the same with a 13-year-old.

Punishing your child: There's no problem punishing a 4-year old. But with a 14-year-old, it's not so easy. Take away their I-Pod and they'll use their Walkman. Take away their Walkman and they'll borrow one from a friend.

Enforcing a punishment: You're in total control when you punish your 5-year-old by refusing to take her to a play date. But punish your 15-year-old with "no chat rooms" and how can you know whether she's sneaking in a conversation while doing her homework? Watching over her to enforce the punishment invariably means more hassles for you than for her.

Without any guilt, a kid will show no remorse for bad behavior. When blamed, she may even go on the offense, holding you responsible for what went wrong.

With neurotic guilt, a kid will feel excessive and inappropriate guilt, undermining his self-esteem and self-confidence.

With healthy guilt, a kid will have internalized appropriate standards of behavior so that he does not need a parent to constantly monitor his activities. He will know when he's done wrong and make amends when it's proper to do so.

Too Much Knowledge,
Not Enough Common Sense

One might be forgiven for thinking that the more one knows, the wiser one would be. Yet, when parents have an abundance of education but only a scintilla of common sense, the results may be quite the opposite.

> "...an abundance of education but only a scintilla of common sense..."

I do not mean to knock parental education. Indeed, it is essential for upgrading your parental skills. However, if the more you learn the more confused you feel and the more you know the more stressed you get, it's time to put the books aside and start relying instead on your own good judgment.

These three guidelines should help you do just that:

Always be mindful that you are the parent.
Keep an open mind toward what your child wants, but not so open that your brains fall out. Families where the kids rule and parents heed is a recipe for disaster. Don't let this happen! If it's already happening, look for every opportunity to assert your authority and regain the parental role.

Being overly child-centered is not a virtue.
Do not end up being a full-time maid, activities coordinator and entertainment planner for your child. If meeting your kids' needs is running you ragged or taking a toll on your marriage, readjust your priorities. Meeting children's needs at the

expense of your sanity is not good child-rearing -
unless your goal is to be the proud parent of a self-
centered narcissist.

The experts say consistency is important.
Yes, to a degree. But, please use your common
sense. Don't pretend that you and your spouse are
clones of each other. Your kids already know
you're not. It's not harmful for kids to know that
mom makes me go to bed at 9 but when dad's in
charge I can stay up later. Avoid undermining each
other's parenting style by making a big deal about
these small differences.

Child rearing is more art than science. Though education can help, it is
not and never will be - the be all and end all. Have faith in your
intuition. Respect your street smarts. Don't sweat the small stuff. And
never, ever lose your sense of humor.

Mother-Daughter Adult Relationships

Now that you're an adult, has your relationship with your mother matured? Or does it seem as if the conflicts and tussles you had a kid are still repeating themselves ad nauseam?

58-year-old Doris and her 32-year-old daughter Danielle have been having the same arguments for the last 15 years. Here's what they say:

Doris: "Danielle hardly ever calls me. When I call her, she takes days to get back to me. She complains that I meddle in her affairs when all I'm trying to do is be helpful. If I offer her advice from my life experiences, she thinks I'm being critical. Can't a mother tell an adult daughter anything?"

Danielle: "My mother gets me so worked up. She's always telling me what I should do. She's very opinionated. If it's not her way, it's not the right way. She gives me the same advice repeatedly and claims she's only doing it because she loves me. It feels more like control than love. If she really loves me, can't she let me live my own life?"

When Danielle grumbles about her mom, her friends validate her take on it:
| *"Your mom's a control freak."* |

"You've got a right to live your life the way you want to. Your mom's a control freak; she should back off."

Yet, when Doris gripes to her friends about her daughter's attitude, she also gets validated: "You've got a right to tell her what you think. After all, you are her mother."

Many parent-child struggles continue *forever*, tainting an otherwise loving relationship. It's easy for this to happen if *both* parties do not update how they relate to each other. Here's some advice to help a mother-daughter relationship evolve:

Advice for Mom:

> Give up the idea that it is your job to set your adult child straight. You may offer your opinion, but remember opinions are your take on the matter; they are not facts. For example, if you believe your daughter could improve her appearance by dressing better, that's your opinion. It's meddling to continue to pressure her to dress the way you think she should. There is a difference between giving your opinion once and repeatedly pressuring your daughter to do things your way. Expect sparks to fly if you do not respect your daughter as a separate being with her own style and mind.

> You may believe that you're inspiring your daughter to do better by comparing her to other people her age. Comparisons like these, however, are hurtful and unfair. They suggest that your daughter is not good enough as is and that the other person is the 'model' daughter. Just imagine how you would feel if your daughter compared you to another mother, suggesting that you should live your life the way that mom does. Doesn't feel too good, does it?

Advice for Daughter:

> Don't be hungry for your mother's approval for everything you do. She may not really understand nor

appreciate the way you live your life. That's okay. As an adult, you shouldn't need her approval or her consent for everything you do. If your mother's words have more impact on you than you would like, it's a good bet that you need to address your own separation issues.

Try not to interpret every comment your mother makes as yet another criticism. It's likely that your mom is feeling powerless in her relationship with you. Giving you advice is one way that she may be holding on to a relationship that is slipping away from her. Taking care of you has been her job for decades. Her remarks may be her way of still looking out for your best interests, as she sees them. Respond by thanking her for her concerns, and then go about your business knowing that you are free to do exactly as you please. Remember, you're an adult now.

PART 5

Dealing with Difficult People

Fasten your seat belts!
You're in for a bumpy ride as you learn how
to deal with difficult people.

Some cause happiness wherever they go; others whenever they go.

Oscar Wilde

Man will do many things to get himself loved; he will do all things to get himself envied.

Mark Twain

How to Argue With a Difficult Person

How do you respond to a difficult person? What can you say to someone who is mouthing off disrespectfully? How can you avoid getting into a shouting match, replying with cheap shots that bring you down to the level of a 5 year old?

First, a **few don'ts**:

> **Don't** name call.
>
> **Don't** curse at the person.
>
> **Don't** become enraged.
>
> **Don't** lose control or spew venom.
>
> **Don't** exaggerate what the other person said. (*"So, you think I'm a complete idiot?"*)
>
> **Don't** answer setup questions. (*"You think you're smarter than me, don't you?"*)
>
> **Don't** expect to change his mind if he is in complete disagreement with you. Trying to get him to "get it" will only increase your frustration.

Now **a few do's** that will help you make your point, whether or not the other person "gets it".

Be curious about how the other person came to think the way he thinks.
Sometimes, it all makes sense once you understand another's background and experience.
("What makes you feel so strongly about this issue?")

Look for a point of agreement.
Even if you differ strongly on 90% of things, there's probably something that you can both agree on. If so, state it respectfully.
("At least, we both recognize that this is a serious matter.")

Make your point with a statement, not a question.
("The way I look at it is...")

Tell a personal story to illustrate your point.
People tend to soften when they listen to such stories.
("My father was in Vietnam and this is what he told me...")

Frame your position in a way that makes sense to you. Don't argue from another's position.
("I'm not against disciplining children; I'm for letting kids learn from their own mistakes.")

If the other person is trying to 'hook you', don't take the bait.
("You bring up a tough issue that I don't want to get into right now.")

End your conversation before you say what you may later regret.
("Clearly we see things differently; we're not going to change each other. So, let's agree to disagree and call it a day.")

We're often under the illusion that if only others understood 'the facts' (as we see them), they'd embrace our position. When they don't, we're perplexed and frustrated. In those moments, it's hard to imagine that they have their own version of 'the facts'. And that what we strongly adhere to may offend their sense of reality and deeply entrenched beliefs. And that just as strongly as we believe we're right, they believe we're wrong.

> **People have their own version of 'the facts'.**

If you're in a tiff with a difficult person, don't escalate the conflict by trying to change him. Simply state what you feel, what you think, what you believe, and then let go.

Dealing With a
Passive-Aggressive Personality

He's kind, caring, and an all-around nice guy – most of the time. Other times, you wonder about him. Doesn't he hear you? Doesn't he care? Is he stubborn, stupid or what?

Like the time you were preparing dinner and asked him if he'd buy a quart of skim milk and a package of American cheese on his way home. He responded "Sure, no problem," but instead brought home whole milk and Swiss cheese. You were left thinking – Hello, is anybody home? I could have sent my 10 year-old to the store with better results!

When you confront him about buying the wrong items, he becomes irritated with you. He says he forgot, doesn't see what the big deal is and accuses you of never being satisfied with anything he does. You alternate between feeling guilty (wondering if indeed you are too finicky or demanding) and feeling frustrated that he can't execute a simple task.

If this scenario seems familiar, it's time to learn more about passive-aggressive personalities.

David appears to be a "nice" guy, both in his personal and professional relationships. If asked to do something, he typically responds, "No problem, I'll get to it," or "I'll get back to you on this." But his follow-through on these matters leaves much to be desired. Hiding his defiance under a guise of compliance, he

> **"He promises anything but then does as he pleases."**

promises anything but then does as he pleases.

David's pattern began in childhood. Not wanting to argue with his parents but wishing to get them off his back, he became well skilled in passive-aggressive strategies, such as:

> *"I'll get to it in a minute, Ma."*
> (But never gave it a second thought.)

> *"I did my homework, Dad."*
> (In fact, he only did his math homework.)

> *"I'm doing my homework right now."*
> (Works for two minutes, then returns to his game.)

> *"Don't worry. I'll take care of that mess in the garage."*
> (Without specifying when.)

> *"Yeah, I'll do it."*
> (But never does.)

> *"That report isn't due till next week."*
> (Puts off responsibilities till the last minute.)

> *"As soon as I finish these other things."*
> (Always has a reason why he can't do it now.)

These childhood behaviors have carried over to David's adult life. To this day, he's still uncomfortable with conflict, unable to negotiate a compromise or refuse a request directly. Instead, his way of getting along is to agree with what another wants, but then does things his own way or simply doesn't do it at all.

What is the effect of passive-aggressive behavior on the other person? In a nutshell, it drives the other person nuts!

It's frustrating to try to communicate with someone you can't pin down.

It's discouraging to try to converse with someone who doesn't give you a straight answer.

It's exasperating to count on someone whose words and actions don't mesh.

It's unnerving to keep hearing yet another never-ending excuse.

If you're involved with a passive-aggressive personality, there'll be times that you'll lose your cool. When you do, he'll tell you to get a grip, acting as though he had no part in the dissension between the two of you.

Once it reaches this stage, he may reverse course becoming overly solicitous of your needs, as you wonder, why, oh why, does it all have to be so difficult?

What can you do to change the pattern? Here's my advice:

Recognize the pattern.
Instead of just feeling guilty, angry or bewildered, label this disconcerting pattern of behavior as passive-aggressive.

Express your anger before you get to the rage stage.
Explain how his action (or lack of action) affects you. Express your feelings without going over the top. Suggest alternative behaviors.

Call the passive-aggressive person on his behavior.
If a promise hasn't been kept, confront him. If his response is evasive, ask him to be clearer about what he means. If he won't give you a straight answer, tell him how his behavioral style is affecting you.

Encourage the passive-aggressive person to express his feelings directly – even negative ones.
Despite some initial discomfort, you may find it refreshing to have open and honest disputes instead of struggling to decipher double messages and oblique communication.

Nix the guilt.
Though you may be a part of the problem, one thing is certain. You're not the sole cause of the problem, nor can you be the sole solution.

When in doubt as to whether you should trust what a passive-aggressive person says, go with your gut.
If, like Hamlet, you're torn between two impulses – "to believe" or "not to believe" – give less importance to what's being said, more importance to what your instincts tell you are true. Keep in mind that the best predictor of future behavior is past behavior.

Dealing With a
Narcissistic Personality

"He just doesn't get it! I don't know how such a smart and talented young man could be so selfish, so dense."

Bill was grumbling about his son. This time, once again, the problem revolved around money. "Mike didn't even ask to borrow money. He told me he needed a new state-of-the-art computer only 6 months after he needed a 'loan' because the lease on his Lexus had expired. Mike wasn't even apologetic when he asked me to foot the bill. He just rattled off a bunch of reasons about why he couldn't be expected to pay for these things and why I should."

Bill continued. "When Mike was a teenager, I used to think he'd outgrow this pattern. But he's 29 years old now and I don't see anything changing. He just wants what he wants and doesn't care how his wants affect me or his mother."

When I suggested to Bill that his son sounded like a narcissist, Bill immediately defended him. "It's not that he doesn't care about us," he retorted. "He can be very loving. He just doesn't have high self-esteem and needs material things to make him feel better about himself."

It's often hard to accept that someone you care for has a narcissistic personality, especially when he (or she) is talented, charming, smart, and yes, even caring at times. Yet, if you are bewildered by your loved one's expectations and repeatedly feel taken advantage of, don't let your wishful thinking stand in the way of reality.

Narcissism is on the rise today, reinforced by our culture that proclaims that "you deserve the best" and "you're worth it", without giving any thought as to why you deserve the best or without making a connection between being worth it and being able to afford it.

> **"Narcissism is on the rise today..."**

Since there is a good chance that there's a narcissist in your life (or perhaps you recognize these traits in yourself), here's some facts you should know about this type of personality.

Narcissists are highly focused on their own needs, giving short shrift to how their needs impact others.

> Mike does not concern himself with what his "needs" cost his parents, even though he knows they are not wealthy people.

Narcissists show little empathy, shrugging off another's perspective with a quick quip.

> When Mike's dad tried to explain to his son that he's feeling burdened by his ongoing expenses, Mike quipped, "hey, you gotta live for today."

Narcissists need continuous validation from others. Feeling empty on the inside, they have an insatiable need for praise from the outside and expertly deflect the criticism they receive.

> When Mike's mom tells him she's disappointed in his unrealistic demands, he puts his arm around her and tells her not to worry.

Narcissists are overly concerned with external appearances and status symbols that enhance their sense of importance.

> Mike feels that he's deserving of a top-of-the line computer and car, regardless of his financial situation.

Narcissists seek out relationships that will feed their ego. Impulsive and impatient, they maintain relationships only if their needs are being met.

> Mike's parents fear that if they cut Mike off financially, he might write them off. Their fears are well grounded in reality.

Narcissists can, at times, by quite generous with others. Their generosity, however, must feed their sense of importance.

> Though Mike doesn't even think about repaying his parents for their "loans", he will treat them to expensive dinners and buy them lavish gifts as a way to build up his self-esteem.

Narcissistic personalities run the gamut from mild to severe. But no matter how mild the syndrome is, you still need to be on guard against being exploited. Here's what how you can protect yourself:

Know in your own mind what your limits are. Then clearly state and enforce those limits. Here are 5 areas that generally need to be addressed:

- **Time** (Don't be at her beck and call to do whatever she wants, whenever she wants it.)
- **Money** (Your money is not her money. Be clear as to what you will and will not pay for.)
- **Possessions** (Be specific about what possessions you will share, if any, and what is off limits.)
- **Conversations** (Interrupt endless talk about the minutiae of the narcissist's life. Segue into conversation that is also of interest to you.)
- **Responsibilities** (Clarify what responsibilities are hers and what are yours. Don't take on her obligations if she "forgets" or has "no time".)

Clarify the consequences for disrespecting boundaries or going over the limits.
You may feel like you're interacting with a child when you do this, but since the narcissist doesn't reflect on how his actions affect you, he is, in many ways, acting like a child.

Stay the course.
Refuse to be blackmailed by temper tantrums, threats, name calling or "I hate you." Do not let yourself be manipulated into rescuing him from the consequences of his irresponsible behavior.

If he tells you, you're the greatest, take it with a grain of salt.
Today, you're the object of his affection; tomorrow, it's just as likely you will be the cause of his woes.

If you believe she's acting inappropriately, say so.
If her expectations are out of line, say so. You must maintain a reasonable perspective on what is; as she cannot be counted on to do so.

Avoid getting sucked into a narcissist's way of thinking, no matter how persuasive or charismatic she may be. For once you're sucked in, you will find yourself in a never ending struggle to just keep your head above water.

Dealing With a
Borderline Personality

We are a psychologically sophisticated society. Emotional diagnoses that most people weren't familiar with a generation ago are now part of our everyday lingo.

Ask a 12-year-old kid if she knows anyone who is anxious, depressed, obsessive, compulsive, phobic or neurotic, and she'll know exactly what you're talking about. Ask her about a borderline personality disorder, however, and she'll look at you quizzically. But then again, it would be unlikely for you to ask that question as you may also be unfamiliar with this syndrome.

Often, borderlines themselves don't even know what their problem is other than being aware that their life is highly turbulent and chaotic.

And yet, borderline personality disorder is so widespread that it's been said that we live in a borderline culture. Watch daytime TV talk shows and you'll know exactly what I mean.

> "Watch daytime TV talk shows and you'll know exactly what I mean."

Since it's a good chance that you may know a borderline (or recognize these traits in yourself), it would be helpful for you to know more about this personality disorder:

-**Borderlines** have unpredictable and rapid mood swings, with episodes of depression and sudden emotional outbursts.

-Borderlines split their world into rigid categories of "good" or "bad", "black or "white". Shades of gray are nonexistent. A friend, a parent, even a therapist is idealized one day, then the next day falls off the pedestal because he did something wrong.

-Borderlines are overly sensitive to being abandoned and rejected, though this doesn't stop them from treating others harshly. They are often abusively critical to those closest to them.

-Borderlines become outraged with little provocation. Consequently, it's difficult for them to maintain a job, keep an intimate relationship or even to remain in therapy.

-Borderlines get anxious when they are alone, as aloneness may trigger terrifying feelings of emptiness. As an antidote to these feelings, they often act out with drinking, drugs, cutting, binging, shoplifting, driving recklessly or promiscuous sex.

For those who live or work with borderlines, life can feel like an emotional roller coaster that simply never comes to a stop.

Consider these two examples:

Personal Example:
You've just been diagnosed with breast cancer. You call Darlene, leaving her a message that you really need to talk to her. She doesn't call back for several days. When she hears the news, she's warm and caring. She invites you to dinner that night. When you refuse, saying "not tonight", you don't hear from Darlene for weeks.

When she finally does call, she's in crisis mode, having had yet another breakup with her boyfriend. She needs you. You remind her of your own crisis. She feels victimized; nobody's there for her, while everybody's supporting you. The conversation ends abruptly. The following week she calls again; this time Darlene's in a good mood. She's made up with her boyfriend. She acts as if nothing has happened between the two of you.

Professional Example:
Rick, your supervisor, publicly humiliates you for making an inconsequential error. He's so angry about it that you wonder whether you're about to be fired.

A week later, he calls you into his office to tell you what a great job you've been doing. His change of heart confuses you. It's not the first time he's been angry one moment, then your chief supporter a short time later. You've tried to talk to him about his inconsistent attitude, but he doesn't acknowledge any of it. This makes you feel even more confused.

Borderline personalities run the gamut from mild to severe. But no matter how mild the syndrome is, it still presents problems for others. If you are involved with a borderline personality, here's what you must do:

Be Consistent - Whatever you have told the borderline you will do (or won't do), keep your word. Be consistent and predictable, even if you need to suffer through a violent outburst of accusations or a tearful meltdown. If you become hostage to these emotional explosions, the borderline gets the upper hand. And if you think you've got problems now, just wait!

Encourage Responsibility - Do not become the borderline's rescuer by becoming responsible for her irresponsible actions. If she racks up bills she can't afford to pay, don't pick up the tab. If his reckless driving totals his car, don't buy him a new one. If he's been fired because he can't get along with people, don't agree with him that he's been a helpless victim of circumstances. The borderline will have no incentive to change, if you keep rescuing him from the consequences of his irresponsible behavior.

Give Honest Feedback – Don't reinforce the borderline's belief that she's been treated unfairly, unless you actually think this is the truth. Don't encourage her righteous indignation. Don't be manipulated into agreeing with her that it's a black and white situation. Speak about shades of gray, even if she doesn't want to hear it.

If you are looking for more information on how to deal with a borderline personality, here are 3 books that will be of invaluable help to you.

Kreisman, Jerold Dr. and Hal Straus, *I Hate You— Don't Leave Me.* New York: Avon, 1991.

Kreisman, Jerold Dr. and Hal Straus, *Sometimes I Act Crazy: Living with Borderline Personality Disorder.* New York: Wiley, *2004.*

Mason, Paul Dr. and Randi Kreger. *Stop Walking on Eggshells: Taking Your Life Back When Someone You Care about Has Borderline Personality Disorder.* Oakland, California: New Harbinger, 1998.

PART 6

The Change Process

You can be the recipient of the best advice, but
if you pay no attention to it,
are you really any better off?

*The journey of discovery begins not with new vistas but with
having new eyes with which to behold them.*

Marcel Proust

*It is not the strongest of the species that survive, nor the
most intelligent, but the one most responsive to change.*

Charles Darwin

Can People Really Change?

Adam's hope was dwindling as he turned to me and said, *"They say that a leopard doesn't change his spots; do you think that people ever really change the way they are?"*

I responded, *"Certainly. As a psychologist, that's what I do - help people change."*

Adam was not the first person to wonder whether people are truly capable of changing. Such a question usually pops up when one is frustrated with another's behavior and has "tried everything" to get that person to change his ways. When nothing makes an impact, the pessimistic conclusion is that change is not possible. So though it's true that people can change, you do need to keep in mind a few basic caveats to ensure that your expectations are realistic.

> **"I've tried everything to get him to change."**

Change is much easier if one is motivated to change.
If one is unmotivated, it is difficult, if not impossible, to force a change just because *you* want it to happen.

Some people find it easier to change than others.
The more rigid and fixed a person's personality is, the more difficult it is for her to embrace change.

Change doesn't take place magically like it does in fairy tales.
Sure, you can fantasize that people can change their

habits the way they change their clothes. Just do it! Snap out of it! Out with the old, in with the new. Kiss a frog and a prince will be yours. Sorry, this is not the way change works in the real world. But you already knew that, didn't you?

Change takes time.
When change happens quickly and dramatically, it rarely lasts. Stimulated by a motivational seminar? Enthralled with an Oprah show? Electrified by a guru? Great! These are wonderful ways to jumpstart change. But keep in mind that meaningful change, like love, must survive the test of time.

Meaningful change usually transitions through several stages:

Lack of Motivation:
In this stage, a person is not interested in changing. If change takes place at all, it's only because of external pressure ("You're making me do this,") not internal motivation ("I want to change.")

Getting Ready to Get Ready Stage:
In this stage, the desire to change is present, but it resides on the back burner. Look closely, however, and you can see that change is on the horizon. Seeking out information on the Internet, reading an article or conversing with others on the relevant topic are all actions that indicate that one is preparing for change.

Ambivalence:
In this stage, the desire to change is clear. However, one may still be ambivalent, seesawing back and forth between wanting to

change and resisting change. It's often easier to gravitate to the path of least resistance. Instead of losing weight, you purchase a new wardrobe. Instead of getting organized, you write a list about what you should do to get organized, telling yourself you'd do it if only you had the time. In this stage, you are knee deep in "yes, but" and "if only" excuses.

Commitment to Change:
Enough talking the talk; you're now ready to walk the walk. You've made the decision. You've found the way. You take whatever action is necessary. You know how easy it is to slip back to your old ways but you're determined not to let that happen. Hence, if you do backtrack, you don't give up. You get back on track, renewing your commitment to change.

Celebrating the Change:
You've done it! You're proud of yourself. You rejoice in the changes you've made. Life is more fulfilling for you now. You wonder what took you so long.

Here are two stories that illustrate these stages.

John's story:
"I ignored my parents when they gave me a hard time about my drinking. I thought they were being unfair to me. When they told me I had to leave the house, I was shocked. I was in 3 different rehab programs before I admitted my problem.

It wasn't easy to give up drinking, but I'm now committed to staying sober. I attend weekly AA meetings and have a sponsor who helps me through the rough patches. When I look back on my drinking days, I'm ashamed of myself and regret what I put other people through – particularly my parents. But I'm also very proud of the changes I've made."

Susan's story:
"I had this terrible habit of always procrastinating. I'd promise myself I'd take care of a task and then never even begin it. I saw myself as lazy. I couldn't help it. That's just the way I was. Then when I started comparing my life with other people my age, I could see that I was languishing because of my constantly putting things off. I began to think that I deserved better. And that better wouldn't happen, unless I changed the way I operated.

It was then that I went to a psychologist to figure out what I was going to do with my life. I felt energized after each session. I've learned a lot about myself. I know how easy it is for me to go back to my old ways but I'm determined not to let that happen. I definitely want to make a better life for myself."

Change for One

Now that you know about how change works, what can you do to if you want somebody else to change?

First, let's look at the approach most people take. You explain to the other person why he should change. It's for his own good. Your reasons make sense. He may even agree with you, saying he'll *try to change,* yet he doesn't. So you tell him again and again. You try everything. You criticize. You nag. You argue. You demand. You yell. You cry. You punish. You withdraw. You try not to care.

And still he doesn't change. What's going on here?

Something you wish weren't true. And yet you know, deep down, that it is true. People don't change when others tell them they should. They change

> **"People don't change when others tell them they should."**

when they, themselves, are motivated to change.

But what makes somebody become motivated to change?

I wish there were a simple answer to that question, but I've yet to find one. I'm often reminded of a young man I knew who quit using heavy drugs only when he narrowly escaped having his arm amputated. Why then, when dying of an overdose was a daily risk factor for him? His explanation: *"Life is hard enough for me with two arms. I can't imagine living with only one; I'd rather be dead."*

Some people really do have to hit rock bottom to change. Or be jolted by their reality. But even a startling reality doesn't work for some people. It's not unusual to see people diagnosed with lung cancer still puffing away. Or a college student threatened with expulsion still refusing to crack open a book.

So, then what should you do if a loved one won't change, despite all your efforts to make it happen?

Here is your best hope:

> **First Step** - Instead of knocking yourself out trying every possible way you can think of to get the other person to change, save your energy. Admit the futility of seeking to change someone who is not open to changing.

> **Second Step** - Decide how **you** will respond differently, (not to force change on the other person) but to take care of yourself. When you do this, the dynamics of your relationship will automatically change.

Consider how this advice worked for Jill. who walked into my office angry and depressed. She described her situation:

> *"I love my husband but our communication is so limited, it's pathetic. I ask him how his day was, he grunts okay, then flips on the TV. I want to talk with him but he has the attention span of a flea. I've asked him to come to therapy with me but he refuses. What can I do?"*

Jill had tried everything she knew to get her husband to be more communicative. In addition to asking him questions, she was forever initiating conversations hoping to get him involved. Figuring that it might be easier for him to talk later at night without the distraction of the kids, she scheduled "talk time" twice a week. The plan was that the two of them would simply sit on the couch and talk about their feelings.

Her plan backfired when it became obvious that Doug felt trapped. Jill dropped the plan, feeling abandoned and unloved.

The first thing I told Jill was that she was trying much too hard to get Doug to change. I suggested that she stop asking him questions, stop initiating conversations, and cut out the "talk time". If she felt the need to talk with someone, she should call her friends or talk to her kids. Since she had expressed a need to do more things, I also suggested she join a gym or find a class that she'd be interested in taking.

Jill's reaction was negative. She was afraid that such changes would increase the distance between the two of them. I reminded Jill that I wanted her to do these things to take care of herself, not to improve the relationship.

She decided to give my suggestions a try. She signed up for a ceramics course, joined a bridge game and saw her friends more often. Within a few weeks time, she noticed that she was feeling less resentful even though Doug, true to form, was still his non-communicative self.

A month later, she was surprised to hear Doug complain about how busy she was with things that did not include him. He admitted to feeling lonely and wanting her to spend more time at home. Jill was careful not to drop her new activities and return to the way things used to be.

Instead, she responded affirmatively, "You're right. I have been out a lot. This weekend, however, would be a good time for us to be together. Anything in particular, you'd like to do or talk about?"

Doug responded, "No, just want to be around you."

Jill smiled, feeling pleased with herself that the "change for one" plan was working. No longer was she actively pursuing Doug, practically begging him to be with her. And though Doug was still deficient in the gift of gab, still reluctant to venture into emotional terrain, she did appreciate that he missed her, loved her and wanted to be around her.

A paradoxical benefit:
The less Jill pressured Doug to talk, the more he opened up. Some things just seem to work out that way.

Psychotherapy - To Know It Is To Appreciate It

Though it happens less frequently than it used to, I still hear people say that they "don't believe" in psychotherapy.

"It's a crutch for weak people."

"If you need it, it proves you're crazy."

"How is a stranger going to help you?"

"Those psychologists are nuttier than you are."

These remarks originate from ignorance or fear – which is understandable if one has had no experience or, worse yet, a bad experience with psychotherapy.

But a positive experience with psychotherapy? Wow, what a life-changing event that can be!

Many start therapy because of the angst, yet once the angst has settled they stay for the growth.

Typical results:

> Building competence and confidence,
> Greater self-esteem,
> Closer relationships,
> Enhanced communication,

NOW I GET IT!

Better parenting,
More rewarding career choices,
Improved decision making.

Amazing! One process – endless possibilities!

How does all this happen?

There's no simple answer to this question as there are many types of psychotherapists and many schools of psychotherapy. What I've found works best for most people is an **educational model** that utilizes the best of these methods:

Cognitive Therapy which highlights changing irrational beliefs and erroneous thinking.

Behavior-Modification Therapy which highlights changing maladaptive behaviors and avoidance patterns.

Gestalt Therapy which highlights acknowledging and accepting all parts of oneself with the goal of living an integrated and creative life.

Psychodynamic Therapy which highlights the influence of relationships, childhood experiences and intrapsychic conflict.

Systems Therapy (family and couple) which highlights the influence of the system (family, community, work) in which you live.

No one school of therapy is best for everyone. It's preferable if your psychologist uses strategies from many models to meet your needs rather than expecting that your needs must fit into your therapist's orientation.

Psychotropic medications, when indicated, are best utilized as an adjunct to psychotherapy, not as the be all or end all of treatment.

An Alternative Approach - Coaching

Recently, life coaching has developed as an alternative approach to enhancing personal performance. Because coaching has been so successful in helping athletes and artists achieve their goals, it has made a rapid expansion into other areas of life.

Coaching is particularly valuable for those who are self starters, emotionally stable and aware of their goals. Here's an example of how coaching may work:

> Let's say that you're a professional, executive or artist. Though you are doing well, you know you're capable of doing even better. Yet, it's not happening. You're not sure if it relates to fear, self-sabotage, procrastination, negative energy, inadequate communication skills, or relationship difficulties.
>
> Think of how helpful it would be if you were able to work with a personal coach who is non-judgmental and objective. Your coach can function as a mentor, motivator, strategist, idea person and taskmaster. She is someone who is knowledgeable about people skills, such as self-presentation and group dynamics as well as business skills, such as marketing strategies and organizational structure.
>
> As you work together, problems are identified. Requisite skills are learned and practiced. Obstacles and fears are identified, managed or eliminated. Options are explored. Action plans are developed and then implemented.

In short: your personal coach insures that you learn what you need to learn to advance your professional and personal goals.

Sounds good, doesn't it?

NOW I GET IT!

Now that you know about the benefits of psychotherapy and coaching, can you still say "you don't believe in it?"

I can understand if this is not the best time for you or you haven't yet found the right person to work with. But I do hope, now that you 'get it', that you will appreciate how the many forms of psychotherapy can be a sensational resource for you.

SHARE THE WEALTH
ENCOURAGE OTHERS TO 'GET IT' TOO

Bulk Discounts of Autographed Books

Discounts start at only 5 copies and increase based on quantity.

Dynamic Speaking Events

Let Dr. Sapadin share her expertise and advice with your organization. Custom designed programs available.

For more information

Visit www.PsychWisdom.com
Write to DrSapadin@aol.com

Printed in the United States
84079LV00004B/105/A